Tennessee

Tennessee

Deborah Kent

Children's Press®
A Division of Grolier Publishing
New York   London   Hong Kong   Sydney
Danbury, Connecticut

Frontispiece: Little River in the Great Smoky Mountains National Park

Front cover: Cumberland Gap National Historical Park

Back cover: A Civil War cannon in Shilo National Military Park, Savannah

Consultant: Mrs. Kassie Hassler, Tennessee State Library

Please note: All statistics are as up-to-date as possible at the time of publication.

Visit Children's Press on the Internet at http://publishing.grolier.com

Book production by Editorial Directions, Inc.

Library of Congress Cataloging-in-Publication Data

Kent, Deborah.
    Tennessee / Deborah Kent.
        144 p. 24 cm. — (America the beautiful. Second series)
    Includes bibliographical references and index.
    Summary : Describes the geography, plants, animals, history, economy, religions,
culture, sports, arts, and people of Tennessee.
    ISBN 0-516-21044-0
    1. Tennessee—Juvenile literature. [1. Tennessee.] I. Title. II. Series.
    F436.3 .K46 2001
    976.8—dc21
                                                00-020930
                                                  CIP
                                                    AC

Acknowledgments

I wish to express my appreciation to the staffs of the Tennessee Historical Society and the Tennessee Department of Tourism for their generous help as I gathered information for this book. Thank you to my reader and research assistant, Natalie Ludena, for her perseverance in hunting up so many vital bits and pieces. I owe special thanks to my sister-in-law, Connie Smith Kent, and to her parents, Richard and Norma Smith, who collected a wealth of material for me and shared their perspective as Chattanooga natives.

A Tennessee farm

Smoky Mountains

Fall Creek Falls

Contents

An iris

Nashville

Chattanooga Choo-choo

Young Tennesseans

A fiddle maker

CHAPTER ONE

The Big Red Curtain

On Friday and Saturday nights, thousands of visitors pack the Grand Ole Opry House in Nashville, Tennessee. Eagerly the crowd watches the big red curtain that hangs in front of the stage. When the curtain rises, the evening's show will get underway at last.

The Grand Ole Opry is a cherished Nashville institution. The longest continuously running radio program in the United States, it has delighted listeners since 1925. The show is a medley of country and bluegrass music, spiced with "cornball" comedy routines. *The Grand Ole Opry* has been broadcast before a live audience from its start. By the 1930s, the program had an enthusiastic national following. Over the years, *The Grand Ole Opry* helped raise country music to the international popularity it enjoys today. It paved the way for Nashville to become the Country Music Capital of the World.

For decades, *The Grand Ole Opry* presented Tennessee as a state full of farmers whose lives revolved around hogs, mules, and pickup trucks. Tennesseans are quick to point out that this image is grossly misleading. Today, most Tennesseans live in towns and cities. They take pride in their state's universities, research cen-

The Grand Ole Opry's current home

Opposite: Maple trees in Fall Creek Falls State Park

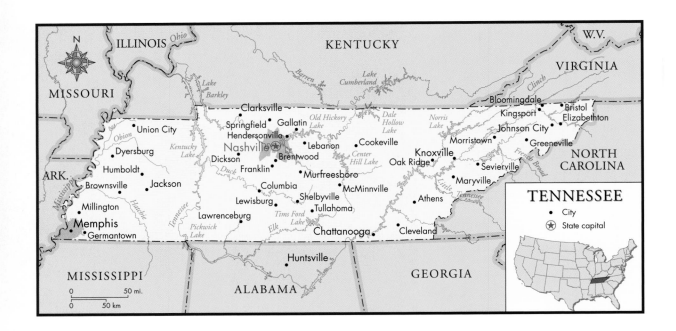

**Geopolitical map
of Tennessee**

ters, and cultural attractions. They honor its long and colorful history and the achievements of its sons and daughters. Tennesseans also treasure the natural wonders of their state—its forests, mountains, rivers, and amazing cave systems.

Stretching from the banks of the Mississippi River in the west to the Great Smoky Mountains in the east, Tennessee lies in the region sometimes known as the Upper South. It is a richly diverse state, blessed with rare natural beauty. Its state and national parks draw millions of people each year.

Even more famous is Tennessee's remarkable musical heritage. Nashville is the heart of the country-music industry. Memphis is home to the haunting musical form known as the blues. And Memphis is the birthplace of rock and roll, as sung by Elvis

Presley, "the King." Tennessee holds a unique place in the story of popular music in the twentieth century.

At the Grand Ole Opry House, the audience waits in restless anticipation. As the big red curtain rises, the crowd bursts into joyous applause—it's showtime!

CHAPTER TWO

The Land of Abundance

"**T**he land is so rich and the soil so deep that in many places one may run a soldier's pike up to the head without meeting a rock or stone, and [it is] capable of producing everything."

—From the journal of a British traveler on the Mississippi River, 1761

The Pinson Mounds were built almost 2,000 years ago.

Caves and Graves

Archaeologists believe that humans reached Tennessee 11,000 years ago. These first Tennesseans were the descendants of people who had come from Siberia into North America. At that time, a land bridge existed across the Bering Strait. In Tennessee, many of the newcomers found shelter in caves along the banks of rivers. Bone fragments and the ashes of long-dead fires show where they cooked their meals.

Over the centuries, groups of people came and went through the Tennessee forests. Some were nomads—they moved from place to place fishing and hunting. Others settled down in villages and

Opposite: Full moon over Cades Cove

raised corn and beans. These farmers learned to make pottery bowls and water bottles, which they decorated with paintings of people and animals.

The prehistoric peoples of Tennessee traded widely. The Mississippi River served as a highway for traders bringing copper from the Great Lakes and shells from the Gulf of Mexico.

Outside the town of Jackson in Madison County stand the Pinson Mounds, a remarkable cluster of earthen structures. The mounds are shaped like the pyramids of ancient Egypt. Each rises in a series of steplike terraces to a flat top. Saul's Mound, the tallest, is 70 feet (21 meters) high. The Pinson Mounds were built nearly 2,000 years ago.

A number of the early groups in Tennessee built earthen mounds such as those in Madison County. These mound-building cultures were the most advanced of Tennessee's prehistoric peoples. Many of the mounds were the graves of chiefs and other important people. The dead were buried with spears, jewelry, and pottery

Exploring the Past at Chucalissa

For almost 700 years, from A.D. 900 to 1600, the Chucalissa Mound was the center of a thriving village. Archaeologists believe that this large, flat-topped mound, located a few miles south of present-day Memphis, was used in the ceremonial worship of a sun god. A broad plaza and a series of huts (left) and smaller mounds surrounded the mound. Today, visitors can learn about the lives of the Mound Builders at the Chucalissa Archaeological Museum. Carefully constructed exhibits offer a glimpse of planting, pottery-making, and other daily activities. Visitors can even climb into an archaeologist's trench to learn how artifacts are removed from the ground. ■

vessels filled with food. Apparently these supplies were intended to serve the dead on their journey to the next world.

By the end of the sixteenth century, the Mound Builders had largely disappeared from Tennessee. Some historians believe they were driven from their homes by enemy tribes. Others suggest epidemic diseases may have destroyed them. No one knows the answer for certain. But, when European settlers reached Tennessee, the Mound Builders were gone, taking their secrets with them.

People of the Forest

During the middle of the sixteenth century, three groups of Native Americans lived in present-day Tennessee. The Creek, who had extensive territory farther south, hunted in the mountainous tip of east Tennessee. The Cherokee lived in much of east and central Tennessee. West Tennessee was the home of the Chickasaw. The Native Americans lived in villages and planted corn, squash, and several kinds of beans. They also fished in the streams and rivers, hunted deer and other game, and gathered wild nuts and berries.

During the summer, the Indians lived in houses made of young trees, woven together and plastered with mud. In the winter, several families shared a large, rectangular house made of logs.

Like the Mound Builders and other early peoples, the Indians traded over a wide territory. They traveled the rivers in long dugout canoes, made by burning a deep hollow into a massive log. They also cut trails through the forest and pounded the land smooth with their moccasin-clad feet. The most famous of these trails became known as the Natchez Trace. Beginning near present-day Nashville,

Part of the original roadway known as the Natchez Trace

it twisted and turned for 400 miles (644 kilometers) to the site of what is now Natchez, Mississippi.

The Cherokee were a powerful tribe with a highly organized governing system. The head chief controlled towns in the present-day states of Georgia, North Carolina, South Carolina, and Tennessee. Cherokee communities in Tennessee have sometimes been called the "Overhill Towns" because they lay across the mountains from the rest of the nation's territory. The largest of the Overhill Towns was Chiaha near present-day Dandridge. Chiaha was known as a "white town," or peace town, where bloodshed was forbidden.

In the late 1600s, a new Indian group called the Shawnee moved into Tennessee and settled in the Cumberland River valley. The Shawnee fought many battles with the Cherokee and Chickasaw. In 1754, the Shawnee were driven north to new territory

The Height of Fashion

Much of what we know about early Cherokee dress comes from written accounts by white explorers. In 1761, Ensign Henry Timberlake, who was a British military officer, described the Cherokee he met in Tennessee. He said they were "of middle stature, of an olive color, tho' generally painted, and their skin stained with gunpowder, pricked into very pretty figures. The hair of their head is shaved, tho' many of the old people have it plucked out by the roots, except a patch on the hinder part of the head, about twice the bigness of a crownpiece [a British coin], which is ornamented with beads, feathers, wampum, stained deer's hair, and suchlike baubles." ■

across the Ohio River. But they launched raids against the Tennessee tribes for the next fifty years.

Warfare was nothing new for the Chickasaw and the Cherokee. They had fought one enemy after another for generations. But their lives underwent staggering changes when still another wave of newcomers swept into Tennessee. The arrival of Europeans transformed life in Tennessee forever.

Crossing the Mountains

Early in 1540, the Cherokee of east Tennessee heard rumors from neighboring tribes to the south. Pale-skinned strangers were making their way from town to town. They rode huge hoofed beasts and carried weapons that crashed like thunder. Wherever they went, these strangers asked for yellow stones. They were so obsessed with these stones that they seemed insane.

The strangers were Spanish soldiers led by the explorer Hernando de Soto. They had come to North America in search of

Cherokee Alphabet

(chart of Cherokee syllabary symbols)

Talking Leaves

As he recovered from a hunting accident, a Cherokee Indian named Sequoyah (1775?–1843) thought about the written papers, or "talking leaves," that helped European Americans communicate with one another. The Cherokee had never had a written language and Sequoyah realized that it could be a powerful tool. For ten years, he worked to develop a system of writing for the Cherokee language.

Sequoyah's system, called a syllabary, contained eighty-six written symbols (left). Each represented one syllable used in the Cherokee language. By memorizing these symbols, any Cherokee could easily learn to read. By the 1830s, newspapers, almanacs, Christian hymnals, and other materials were being printed in Cherokee. Sequoyah had developed the first known written system for any Native American language. The Cherokee Nation maintains the Sequoyah Birthplace Museum near Vonore, Tennessee, in his honor. ■

gold. Hernando de Soto is regarded as the first European to set foot in Tennessee.

With 600 men, de Soto landed on the Florida coast in the spring of 1539. It took his expedition more than a year to make its way northward through the tangled forests to the Cherokee town of Chiaha, where the Spaniards remained for three weeks. They demanded food, gold, and information.

When de Soto left Chiaha, he and his men headed south down the French Broad River to present-day Knoxville. They continued on a long trek south and west for the next two years, finally reaching the Mississippi River near what is now Natchez, in Mississippi.

The Spaniards spent little time in Tennessee, but they left a terrible legacy of smallpox, measles, diphtheria, and many other dis-

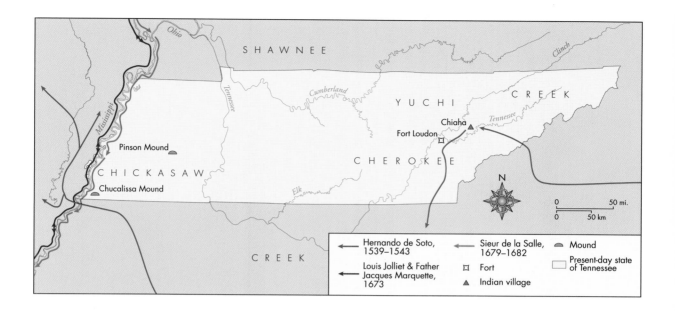

eases. The Indians had never been exposed to these illnesses so they had no natural immunities. Long after the Spaniards left, epidemics swept from village to village, devastating the native peoples.

More than a century passed before Europeans once more touched Tennessee soil. In 1673, two explorers sailed down the Mississippi River in birchbark canoes. One was a French priest, Father Jacques Marquette, who hoped to convert the Indians to Christianity. The other was Louis Jolliet of Canada, who had come to trade with the Indians for valuable furs. Marquette and Jolliet traveled along the western edge of Tennessee and went farther south to present-day Arkansas.

That same summer, two Englishmen entered Tennessee from the east. James Needham and Gabriel Arthur worked for Abraham Wood, a businessman in the English colony of Virginia. Wood wanted Needham and Arthur to explore the country west of the Allegheny Mountains and develop the fur trade with the Indians. The Cherokee captured Needham and Arthur soon after they

Father Jacques Marquette and Louis Jolliet were among the first Europeans to explore what is now Tennessee.

entered present-day Tennessee. The Indians shot Needham and prepared to burn Arthur at the stake. However, Arthur faced death so bravely that the Indians spared his life. He spent a year with the Cherokee, hunting, fishing, and learning the rivers and mountains.

When Arthur finally made his way back to the English colony of North Carolina, he gave excited accounts of the riches to be found in Tennessee. Its streams were home to thousands of beavers, whose glossy pelts would make expensive coats and hats for English gentlemen. Foxes, mink, otters, and other animals were also waiting to make traders rich.

In the decades that followed, the "long hunter" became a fixture in the Overhill country. The long hunters were so named because they made the long journey over the mountains into what are now

For the Glory of Spain

By the time he explored southeastern North America, Hernando de Soto (1500?–1542) had twice won fame and fortune. He had conquered much of Central America and had served for a time as royal governor of Cuba. He had also helped conquer the powerful Inca people of Peru, taking much of their gold and silver for the Spanish king. In North America, however, de Soto's luck ran out. He found no more gold, but only hunger, disease, and war with the Indians. For three years, he wandered from Florida to Tennessee, across Alabama and Mississippi, and down the Mississippi River to Louisiana. Weakened and discouraged, de Soto died and was buried on the banks of the Mississippi so that Indians wouldn't know of his death. ■

Tennessee and Kentucky. They hunted deer, whose hides were sold to make breeches and jackets. The long hunters also traded with the Indians. They exchanged guns, kettles, blankets, knives, mirrors—and sometimes rum—for the pelts of beavers and other animals. The hides and furs were loaded onto packhorses and carried to Charleston, South Carolina. From Charleston, they were shipped to markets in Europe.

The French also sought to gain power and influence in Tennessee. In 1682, a French explorer, René-Robert Cavelier, Sieur de la Salle, claimed the Mississippi Valley for France. La Salle gave this sprawling territory the name New France. In 1714, a French officer, Charles Charleville, established a trading post at French Lick near today's Nashville. However, the English outnumbered the French by as much as twenty to one in Tennessee.

During the 1700s, France and England fought a series of wars in Europe. The fighting spilled over to North America in a string of conflicts called the French and Indian Wars. In this warfare, France and England struggled for control of trade and territory on the American frontier. Both nations gathered Indian allies, drawing the Cherokee and other tribes into the conflict.

The British began construction of Fort Loudoun, their westernmost fort in the Americas, on the banks of the Little Tennessee River in 1756. The fort was built of thick, upright logs and surrounded by a trench, much like the moat around a European

Fort Loudoun was built in 1756 along the Tennessee River.

castle. To protect the fort, twelve cannon were transported across the mountains. One officer wrote about this laborious project: "[The trader in charge] contrived to poise on each horse a cannon crossways over the pack saddle, and lashed them round the horse's body with belts; but as these horses had to cross a country full of high mountains, and these covered with forests, it would happen that sometimes one end of a cannon would catch a tree, twist upon the saddle and draw the horse down, some of which had by these accidents their backs broken under the weight, and lost their lives; the longest journey those horses could make was 6 miles [10 km] a day."

Fort Loudoun was doomed almost from the start. Urged on by the French, the Cherokee surrounded the fort in the spring of 1760. Supplies of food and water ran low within the stockade, and reinforcements from the Carolinas failed to appear. The soldiers and their families had to eat horse meat. At last, the commanding officer, Captain Paul Demere, surrendered. A few days later, the Indians killed Demere by stuffing his mouth with soil. His captors chanted, "You want land? We will give it to you!"

The defeat at Fort Loudoun had little effect on the outcome of the war, however. In 1763, the Treaty of Paris granted Great Britain all of the territory east of the Mississippi River. Tennessee was now in British hands.

Under the Shadows

"You have bought a fair land, but there is a cloud hanging over it.
You will find its settlement dark and bloody."

—Dragging Canoe, a Cherokee war chief, at the signing of
the Treaty of Sycamore Shoals, 1775

The Road to Statehood

With the French and Indian Wars at an end, people from the British
colonies along the Atlantic coast began to push west in search of
more land. Bands of colonists from Virginia, North Carolina, and
South Carolina crossed the mountains to settle in east Tennessee.
In 1769, William Bean built a log cabin on Boone's Creek near the
Watauga River. His son, Russell Bean, was the first white child
born in the Tennessee territory.

Bean's cabin became the hub of a lively settlement as more pioneers moved to the Watauga Valley. Other settlements sprang up along the nearby Carter and Nolichucky Rivers. In 1772, the settlers organized a democratic government under the Watauga Association. The Watauga settlement was incorporated into the British colony of North Carolina in 1777. This "overmountain" portion of North Carolina was called Washington County. With its capital at Jonesboro, Washington County covered nearly all of what is now Tennessee.

The Cherokee deeply resented the growing presence of these intruders on their land. Cherokee raiding parties attacked settlers and burned their crops and cabins. In 1775, a North Carolina land speculator named Richard Henderson negotiated the Treaty of Sycamore Shoals. The treaty allowed Henderson's Transylvania Company to purchase an immense tract of Cherokee land. The company paid the Indians about $50,000 in guns, powder, and other goods. Bitter over the land sale, some Cherokee joined the war chief Dragging Canoe to continue fighting the settlers.

The Transylvania Company encouraged pioneer families to emigrate to the newly opened territory. It established new settlements in the Cumberland Valley of middle Tennessee. In 1780, the company founded the town of Nashborough, which grew rapidly. Its name was eventually changed to Nashville.

While settlers struggled for survival on the frontier, momentous changes were occurring among the British colonies in the east. In 1776, during the Revolutionary War (1775–1783), delegates from the thirteen colonies signed the Declaration of Independence. The declaration stated that the colonies were breaking their ties with

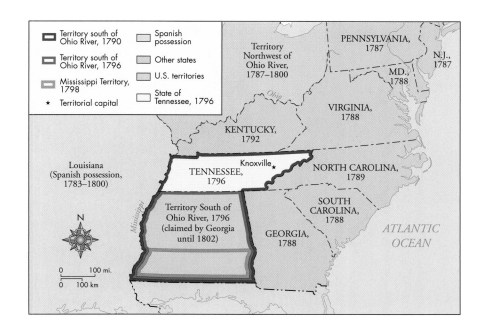

Legend:
- Territory south of Ohio River, 1790
- Territory south of Ohio River, 1796
- Mississippi Territory, 1798
- ★ Territorial capital
- Spanish possession
- Other states
- U.S. territories
- State of Tennessee, 1796

Territory Northwest of Ohio River, 1787–1800

Ohio

PENNSYLVANIA, 1787

N.J., 1787

MD., 1788

VIRGINIA, 1788

KENTUCKY, 1792

Louisiana (Spanish possession, 1783–1800)

Mississippi

TENNESSEE, 1796

Knoxville ★

NORTH CAROLINA, 1789

Territory South of Ohio River, 1796 (claimed by Georgia until 1802)

SOUTH CAROLINA, 1788

GEORGIA, 1788

ATLANTIC OCEAN

N

0   100 mi.
0   100 km

Historical map of Tennessee

Great Britain, the mother country, to become an independent nation. The war raged on for seven more years.

For the most part, the colonists favored independence from Great Britain. A number of "Overmountain men" joined the colonial rebels fighting in Virginia and the Carolinas. In September 1780, British Major Patrick Ferguson began marching west with 1,200 troops to crush the Overmountain men. Learning of Ferguson's plans, Watauga colonel John Sevier and Indian fighter William Campbell mustered resistance.

Under Sevier, Campbell, and Colonel Isaac Shelby, the Overmountain men headed east on a ten-day march, gathering more supporters as they went. The Tennessee troops met Ferguson on a wooded South Carolina ridge called Kings Mountain. Experienced in backwoods fighting tactics, the Overmountain men fired from

Tennessee troops fought in the Battle of Kings Mountain.

behind trees and bushes. The mounted British soldiers, defending the ridge in military formation, were easy targets.

Ferguson and nearly half of his men were killed, while only twenty-eight Tennessee men lost their lives. The Battle of Kings Mountain marked a turning point in the war in the southern colonies.

In 1783, the British were finally defeated. The Overmountain settlements were part of a new nation—the United States of America.

Though the war with Great Britain was over, the bloodshed went on in Tennessee. Chickamauga raiding parties continued to attack settlers. In 1784, the Watauga Association asked the North Carolina government for protection. But North Carolina was unwilling to send troops to help frontier outposts hundreds of miles away. Instead, the state gave the Overmountain region to the new U.S. government in payment for some of its war debts.

Outraged by North Carolina's treatment, the Overmountain settlers petitioned for statehood. Delegates met in Jonesboro and drafted a constitution. They chose the name Franklin, after the inventor and patriot Benjamin Franklin. The people of Franklin called themselves Franklanders. As governor, the Franklanders elected Colonel John Sevier, hero of the Battle of Kings Mountain.

Jonesboro served as a meeting place for the Overmountain settlers.

Chucky Jack

In the story of early Tennessee, one name appears over and over—that of John Sevier (1745–1815). Born in Virginia, Sevier brought his wife and children to the Watauga settlements in the 1770s.

Sevier quickly earned respect as an Indian fighter in the wars with the Chickamauga. He is also remembered as the heroic leader of the Overmountain men at the Battle of Kings Mountain. His men called him "Chucky Jack" because he had a farm on the Nolichucky River.

After the war, Sevier turned to politics. He served as the only governor of the "Lost State of Franklin." In 1796, he became Tennessee's first governor, and he was reelected five times. He also spent four terms in Washington as a congressman representing Tennessee. One acquaintance wrote of Sevier, "Of books he knew little. Men, he had studied well and accurately."

Knoxville became the capital of the Tennessee territory in 1792.

Franklin functioned as an independent state, but the U.S. Congress never admitted it to the Union. In 1788, Franklin's government collapsed, and North Carolina again claimed the territory. The federal government took control once more in 1790, creating the Southwest Territory. Knoxville was chosen as territorial capital in 1792.

The people of the Southwest Territory drew up a new constitution and petitioned for statehood in January 1796. Congress admitted Tennessee to the Union on June 1, 1796, as the sixteenth state.

Becoming a State

Delegates met in Knoxville to draw up a state constitution in January 1796. They named the new state "Tennessee" after *Tenasie*, a Cherokee village. While they waited for Congress to approve the constitution, the Tennesseans elected a governor—John Sevier; two U.S. senators; and a congressman. On June 1, 1796, Congress admitted Tennessee to the Union as the sixteenth state. However, it refused to seat the senators and congressman who had been elected before statehood became official. Tennessee held its elections a second time. The representatives were reelected and sent to Washington. ■

The Widening Reach

After statehood, more and more settlers flooded into east and middle Tennessee. Their favorite route took them through the Cumberland Gap, a passage through the mountains north of Knoxville. Some of the settlers came on foot. Some came on horseback, or leading mules packed with all their worldly possessions. Some arrived in lumbering Conestoga wagons pulled by teams of horses with jingling bells on their harnesses. Soon the wilderness was broken up into farmers' fields, and hard-packed dirt roads crisscrossed the forests.

In 1818, the U.S. government bought a large tract of land from the Chickasaw. This purchase extended Tennessee from the Cumberland Valley west to the Mississippi. The following year, a new town was

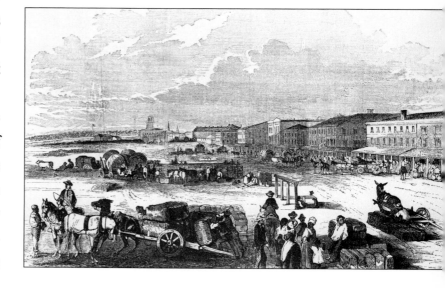

Unloading bales of cotton in Memphis

founded as a port on the river. Because the Mississippi was sometimes compared to the Nile River in Egypt, the new port was named for an ancient Egyptian city—Memphis.

Most of the people who settled east and middle Tennessee were small farmers. They worked the land themselves, or with the help of a few servants. In contrast, the people who settled west Tennessee purchased large tracts of rich, fertile land. This "delta" land was excellent for growing cotton. In Tennessee, as in other southern states, African-American slaves did all the work on cotton plantations. Thus, slavery became part of the economy and the way of life in west Tennessee.

Most Americans regarded Tennessee as a rugged frontier state, its people scratching out a living from farms in the mountains. Yet, to the nation's amazement, a rough-hewn Tennessean swept the presidential election of 1828 and vaulted into the White House. Andrew Jackson campaigned as a man of the common people. Jackson was the first U.S. president born in a log cabin. He showed the American people that a person could rise from humble beginnings to the highest office in the land.

Jackson was also a firm believer in the expansion of U.S. territory and had little regard for the claims and rights of the Native Americans. In 1830, he signed the Indian Removal Act, which required the Cherokee to give up their land and move west of the Mississippi. In 1838, U.S. troops rounded up the Cherokee in Georgia and east Tennessee. Some 14,000 Cherokee—women, men, and children—began a forced march of 1,200 miles (1,931 km) to the treeless plains of Oklahoma. Food was scarce on the march, and the Indians did not even have blankets to protect them

Old Hickory

Born on the Carolina frontier, Andrew Jackson (1767–1845) moved to Nashville to practice law in 1788. In 1796, he was elected Tennessee's first congressman. He was elected to the U.S. Senate in 1797. Jackson put on a uniform when the United States fought Great Britain in the War of 1812 (1812–1815). He won national fame when he led his troops to victory in the Battle of New Orleans in 1815.

Jackson's men nicknamed him "Old Hickory" because he was as indestructible as the wood of a hickory tree.

As president, Jackson defended the Union and opposed laws that would give more power to the individual states. One early biographer described him as "the most American of Americans—an embodied Declaration of Independence—the Fourth of July incarnate." ■

from the winter gales. By the time they reached Oklahoma, some 4,000 Cherokee had died. That long, terrible march to Oklahoma is remembered as the Trail of Tears.

A group of Cherokee on the Trail of Tears

King of the Wild Frontier

David "Davy" Crockett (1786–1836) was a legend in his own time, and remains part of American folklore today. According to the stories, he killed a bear when he was three years old and once rode an alligator down Niagara Falls. The real-life Davy Crockett was born in Greene County and spent most of his life in Tennessee. He served as a U.S. congressman from 1827 to 1831 and again from 1833 to 1835. Crockett was known as a crack marksman, a "straight shooter" in the woods. He died heroically at the Battle of the Alamo in the war for Texas independence. ■

America's hunger for land led to war with Mexico in 1846. U.S. troops marched south to claim the disputed territory of Texas. When Tennessee was ordered to provide 2,800 recruits, some 25,000 young Tennesseans volunteered to go to war. Their eagerness earned Tennessee its nickname—the Volunteer State.

The Mexican War was fought far to the south in a foreign country. But, in a few short years, blood flowed on the soil of Tennessee in a war that tore the state and the nation to pieces.

Brother against Brother

By 1860, about 25 percent of all Tennesseans were African-Americans living in slavery. Slavery existed throughout the state, but the greatest number of slaves worked on farms in middle and west Tennessee. In west Tennessee, slaves actually outnumbered free white persons, making up about 60 percent of the total population.

During the 1830s and 1840s, the question of slavery aroused heated debate across the United States. Eventually most of the northern states declared slavery illegal within their borders. But

The Man from Maury County

The Mexican War was fought during the presidency of James K. Polk (1795–1849), a former Tennessee governor. Born in North Carolina, Polk moved with his family to Maury County, Tennessee, when he was eleven years old. For several years, he practiced law in Murfreesboro. Polk was elected to the U.S. Congress in 1825. He served four terms in the House of Representatives and one in the Senate. Polk was elected governor of Tennessee in 1839 and held the office until 1841. In 1844, he won the presidential election in a surprise upset.

A lifelong admirer of Andrew Jackson, Polk wanted the United States to gain as much land as possible. At the end of the Mexican War, the country acquired California, Nevada, Utah, most of Arizona, and parts of Colorado and Wyoming. The United States gained more territory under Polk than under any other president until Alaska was purchased from Russia in 1867. The nation now stretched from the Atlantic Ocean to the Pacific Ocean. ∎

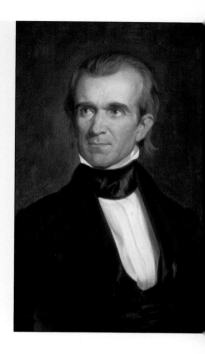

slavery was woven into the fabric of southern life. Most southerners, especially those with money and power, resented the "abolitionists" who argued that slavery should be outlawed forever.

Tension over the slavery issue reached the breaking point in 1861, when South Carolina seceded from the Union. One after another, ten other southern states followed South Carolina's lead.

Like Andrew Jackson, many Tennesseans were deeply loyal to the Union. Others, especially those in slaveholding west Tennessee, sympathized with the rebellious South. They urged Tennessee to join the newly formed Confederate States of America. Tennessee finally broke its ties with the United States on June 8, 1861. It was the last of the southern states to secede.

With the secession of the southern states, the shattered nation

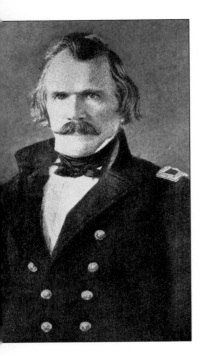

Johnston was a
general in the
Confederate army.

plunged into civil war. Tennessee was deeply divided throughout the war years. As many as 135,000 Tennessee volunteers put on gray uniforms and fought for the Confederacy. Another 70,000, including 20,000 African-Americans, wore the blue uniform of the Union army. Some families were torn apart by conflicting loyalties. In Tennessee, brother literally fought against brother.

For four long years, the war swept back and forth across Tennessee. Altogether 454 battles and skirmishes were fought in the state. Only Virginia was the scene of more military action.

Early in the war, Confederate general Albert Sidney Johnston set up a line of defenses to protect Tennessee from Union invaders. But Johnston's forts were not strong enough to hold back the Union assault. In February 1862, Union general Ulysses S. Grant captured Fort Donelson on the Cumberland River and Fort Henry on the Tennessee. Thousands of Tennesseans fled before the advancing Union troops. U.S. president Abraham Lincoln declared Tennessee under martial law. He placed Brigadier General Andrew Johnson, a Tennessean who remained loyal to the Union, in charge of the state. Johnson set up his military headquarters in Nashville.

In April 1862, General Grant and five divisions of Union troops camped on the Tennessee River near Shiloh Church at the town of Pittsburgh Landing. On the peaceful Sunday morning of April 6, Grant's men heard the rumble of gunfire in the distance. Confederate forces swept down on the Union troops, taking them completely by surprise. Soon the fields were strewn with dying men and horses, and the air rang with screams and groans. The fighting lasted throughout the day and into the next afternoon.

At first, the Confederates appeared to be winning the battle. But

The charge of General Grant at the Battle of Shiloh

after their general bled to death from a wound in his thigh, the troops grew discouraged. The Confederates finally retreated into Mississippi. The Battle of Shiloh is considered a Union victory, but casualties on both sides were appalling. Dragging Canoe's prediction had come true.

In June 1862, Union forces seized Memphis, a key to control of the Mississippi River. Tennessee now lay almost wholly in Union hands. Confederate cavalry forces under Nathan Bedford Forrest and John Hunt Morgan bedeviled the Union ranks with a series of lightning-quick raids. In December 1862, Union and Confederate forces fought at Stones River near Murfreesboro. After three days of bloodshed, the Confederates withdrew, and both sides claimed victory.

The Battle of Lookout Mountain

In 1863, after victory at the Battle of Chickamauga, Confederate general Braxton Bragg laid siege to the Union troops in Chattanooga. Union general Thomas Hooker drove the Confederates back in the Battle of Lookout Mountain. After two days of fighting, Chattanooga remained in Union hands.

In 1864, Andrew Johnson was elected to serve as U.S. vice president under Abraham Lincoln. The Treaty of Appomattox Court House, Virginia, officially ended the Civil War on April 9, 1865. Five days later, before the war-weary nation had a chance to celebrate, John Wilkes Booth shot Lincoln while he attended

Remembering Shiloh

Covering 4,000 acres (1,620 ha) near Pittsburgh Landing on the Tennessee River, Shiloh National Military Park commemorates the Union and Confederate soldiers who fought at the Battle of Shiloh in 1862. Casualties were almost the same for each side— about 1,700 dead and 8,000 wounded. Visitors to the park can walk among rows of headstones bearing the names of the dead from both the South and the North (above). Monuments and plaques mark the battle's major turning points. A short film recounts the battle and its grisly aftermath. ■

a play in Washington, D.C. Lincoln died early the following morning.

The nation staggered under the recent horrors of the war and the shock of Lincoln's death. In this hour of crisis, leadership fell to Andrew Johnson. On the shoulders of this Tennessean lay the responsibility to heal the nation's wounds.

CHAPTER FOUR

In Search of Unity

When midnight shrouds the sacred spot
Where traitors 'gainst their country plot,
What man is damned the first and most,
Damned while they tremble lest his ghost
Should haunt them with a hangman's knot,
And visions grim of gallows-post?

—From a poem by William G. Brownlow,
Tennessee's first governor after the Civil War

Long after the Civil War battles were over, division continued between the North and South.

Rising from the Ashes

William G. Brownlow (1805–1877) was a fiery Methodist preacher and the editor of a Knoxville newspaper. During the Civil War, "Parson" Brownlow staunchly supported the Union cause. When he became governor of Tennessee in the spring of 1865, Brownlow

Opposite: A one-man sit-down demonstration at a segregated lunch counter in 1960

gave a stirring speech to the state legislature in Nashville. He praised the Tennesseans who had fought for the Union and denounced those who had served the Confederacy. He warned the legislature to "guard the ballot-box against treason." According to Brownlow, Tennesseans who had betrayed the Union should not be allowed to vote.

At the close of the Civil War, Tennessee remained a deeply divided state. Union supporters remembered that rebel soldiers had burned and looted their homes. Confederate sympathizers did not forget that soldiers in blue had trampled their crops and stolen their horses. Families from both sides mourned loved ones who had died on the battlefield or perished from disease behind the lines. The war was over, but its bitterness lived on.

President Abraham Lincoln had hoped to heal the nation's terrible wounds. He wanted to bring the southern states back into the Union as quickly as possible. Andrew Johnson tried to carry out Lincoln's Reconstruction policies. But many Americans felt that the defeated Confederates should be punished. They should be stripped of their property and denied the right to vote.

On July 24, 1866, Tennessee became the first Confederate state readmitted to the Union. To qualify for readmission, Tennessee had to ratify, or approve, two new amendments to the U.S. Constitution. The Thirteenth Amendment abolished slavery, and the Fourteenth Amendment gave African-American men the right to vote. (Neither white nor black women could vote until 1920.)

In the late 1860s, most Unionists from east Tennessee joined the Republican Party. White voters in middle and west Tennessee favored the Democrats. East Tennessee accounted for only one-

The President Who Never Went to School

Andrew Johnson (1808–1875) was born in a log cabin in North Carolina. He grew up in poverty, and never attended school. In 1826, Johnson set up a tailor shop in Greeneville, Tennessee. Soon he went into politics and was elected town alderman at the age of twenty.

Johnson was elected to the U.S. Congress in 1843, served as governor of Tennessee from 1853 to 1857, and entered the Senate in 1857. In 1864, Johnson became Lincoln's vice president. When Lincoln was assassinated, the tailor from Greeneville found himself in the White House.

As president, Andrew Johnson tried to bring the southern states smoothly back into the Union. Many in Congress felt that he was much too lenient with the former rebels. A group of his opponents opened impeachment procedures in an effort to remove him from office. Johnson was the first U.S. president ever to undergo an impeachment trial. At the close of the trial, Congress voted to acquit Johnson of the charges against him. The count was so close that Johnson was spared from losing his presidency by only one vote. ∎

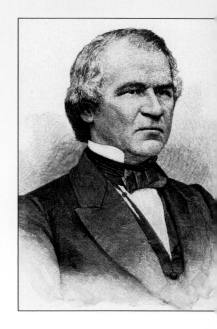

third of the state's potential voters, but the Republicans controlled the legislature. They strengthened their position by denying the vote to former "traitors"—Confederates. They also received the votes of most former slaves.

Whites in middle and west Tennessee were deeply resentful. Some white men fought back by forming a secret society called the Ku Klux Klan. The Klan spread terror by threatening and attacking former slaves, or freedmen. Klansmen were especially unforgiving toward those who "did not know their place," aspiring to gain education, property, and political power.

In the years after the Civil War, former slaves struggled to build new lives of dignity and independence. The Freedmen's Bureau, sponsored by the federal government, opened schools and colleges for African-Americans throughout the southern states.

Men in Hoods

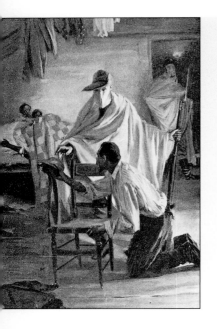

One night in December 1865, six Confederate veterans met in an empty law office in Pulaski, Tennessee. At this meeting they founded a club styled after a college fraternity. Members of the Ku Klux Klan, as the new club was called, put on white robes and hoods and rode through the countryside at night. They knocked down fences, set fire to haystacks, and generally made themselves a nuisance. As white and black Republicans gained power, the Klan expanded, and its activities became more sinister. With Confederate general Nathan Bedford Forrest as its "Grand Wizard," the Klan spread terror through the African-American community. Hooded riders beat blacks and hanged them from trees. Forrest disbanded the Klan after the Republicans lost power in 1869 but the organization has resurfaced many times, carrying on its grim secret activities in the name of white supremacy. ■

By 1880, about 10 percent of Tennessee's former slaves had purchased land and set up their own farms. The vast majority, however, were not so fortunate. Many worked for wages on farms owned by former slaveholders. Some white landowners rented parcels of land to farmhands. The laborers worked in the farmers' fields and then tended their own tiny plots. This system, known as sharecropping, spread across middle and west Tennessee.

Sharecroppers' wages were low and their rents were high. These "tenant farmers" quickly fell into debt, owing more and more money to the landlord they worked for. The sharecroppers toiled for endless hours and fell deeper into debt with each passing year. For both black and white farm laborers, sharecropping was another form of slavery.

African-Americans and some impoverished whites also lost

political ground in the 1870s and 1880s. As the Democrats gained strength, they stripped the blacks of their newly gained rights. New state laws required voters to pay a "poll tax," which few blacks or white sharecroppers could afford. Sometimes voters had to pass a literacy test, which was impossible for people who had never been to school. By 1890, most blacks in Tennessee no longer had any way to take part in the political process. It would be more than seventy years before the promise of freedom was fulfilled.

Conflicts and Promises

For six months in 1897, Tennesseans flocked to Nashville to attend their state's Centennial Exposition. As they wandered among the exhibits they looked back over the state's 100-year history and found ample reason to take pride. Tennessee had tamed a rugged wilderness, and it had survived the bloodshed of the Civil War. Since the war, it had paid off much of its debt. A 3-mile (4.8-km) bridge, opened in 1892, now spanned the Mississippi River at Memphis. And, as proof that the bitter wounds of the war had begun to heal, the Chickamauga and Chattanooga National Military Park had opened in 1895. Monuments in the park honored the courage and sacrifice of both Confederate and Union soldiers.

Tennesseans had also seen hard times in the postwar years, however. The nation's increased demand for coal led to the opening of coal mines on Tennessee's Appalachian Plateau. Conditions in the mines were often brutal, and the miners earned barely enough to keep alive. Some miners tried to form labor unions to press for better pay.

In 1891, owners of the Tennessee Coal, Iron, and Railway

Rockwood's Iron Works in 1879

Company tried to force workers to sign a "yellow dog contract." Such a contract forbade the workers to unionize. Outraged, the workers walked out on strike. The company responded by leasing convicts from state prisons to do the strikers' jobs. Forced to work under guard, these convicts were virtually slaves. Strikers attacked the convicts' guards at Coal Creek, Tracy City, and several other sites. The state militia finally broke the strike. Publicity over the Coal Creek strike helped bring attention to the convict leasing system. It did not end, however, until 1935.

African-Americans met crushing setbacks in the years after the Reconstruction era. Like the rest of the southern states, Tennessee established a code of written and unwritten rules known as the Jim Crow Laws. The Jim Crow Laws enforced a rigid system of racial segregation. Blacks and whites rode in separate cars on trains. They drank from separate drinking fountains, were treated in separate hospitals, and sent their children to separate schools. In most instances, the facilities for blacks were sadly inferior to those for whites.

In 1917, the United States was swept into the appalling conflict known today as World War I (1914–1918). More than 100,000 Tennesseans volunteered for military service. Once again Tennessee lived up to its nickname, the Volunteer State. Most of the Tennessee recruits fought on the battlefields of faraway Europe. They returned home changed forever. They had witnessed the horrors of war, but they had also seen a wider world.

Promises Fulfilled

During the first decades of the twentieth century, Tennessee underwent remarkable changes. New schools and libraries sprang up in

The Horror of the Century

In the stifling summer of 1878, people in Memphis, Tennessee, began to sicken and die of a disease called yellow fever. Yellow fever is spread by mosquitoes, which flourished in the steaming marshes along the Mississippi. The epidemic killed some 5,000 people in Memphis and spread such terror that another 25,000 fled for their lives. The city was forced to declare bankruptcy and lose its charter, which was not reinstated until 1893. A Memphis newspaper editor described the yellow fever epidemic as "the horror of the century, the most harrowing episode in the history of the English-speaking people in America." ■

The Monkey Trial

In the summer of 1925, the nation focused on the little town of Dayton, Tennessee. A high-school science teacher named John T. Scopes was on trial for teaching the theory of evolution, which claims that human beings evolved from lower life forms such as apes. Such teaching violated the Butler Act, a new Tennessee law. According to the Butler Act, the public schools must not challenge the biblical story of divine creation. The American Civil Liberties Union (ACLU) believed the Butler Act violated the separation of church and state as it is set forth in the U.S. Constitution.

Thousands of spectators flocked to Dayton to watch the "Monkey Trial," as it was dubbed by the newspapers. In front of the courthouse, vendors sold monkey pictures, monkey mugs, and rubber monkeys on sticks. The trial pitted two of the nation's leading lawyers against each other. Clarence Darrow (1857–1938) (left) argued in Scopes's defense. William Jennings Bryan (1860–1925) (right) argued for the prosecution. Scopes was found guilty and fined $100. Exhausted by the trial, Bryan died in Dayton five days later. The Tennessee courts upheld the Butler Act, which remained on the books until 1967. ■

cities and towns. Paved highways fanned out across the state, bringing Tennesseans closer together and connecting them with the rest of the world.

Tennessee was hit hard by the disastrous economic depression that gripped the United States in the 1930s. Prices for produce and manufactured goods plummeted and thousands of Tennesseans lost their jobs.

In 1933, one of the Great Depression's worst years, President Franklin D. Roosevelt proposed an ambitious program to produce hydroelectric power from the Tennessee River. Roosevelt created the Tennessee Valley Authority (TVA) "for the proper use, conservation, and development of the natural resources of the Tennessee River drainage basin and its adjoining territory for the general social and economic welfare of the Nation." Over the years, the TVA built a series of dams along the river. The river was harnessed to produce electricity, water crops, and provide summer recreation.

The Norris Dam was the first of the dams to be finished by the Tennessee Valley Authority.

When the United States went to war again in 1941, thousands of Tennesseans once more volunteered to join the armed forces. On the home front, Tennessee also supported the war effort. About 200,000 Tennesseans worked in war plants, making uniforms, airplane parts, and other military equipment. In 1942, the federal government began construction of a top-secret facility on the Clinch River in Roane and Anderson Counties. The city of Oak Ridge sprang up almost overnight to house scientists, engineers, and other workers. By the end of the war, Oak Ridge was home to about 75,000 people. Oak Ridge scientists purified uranium for use in the atomic bombs that were dropped on Hiroshima and Nagasaki, Japan, in 1945.

After World War II, more and more Tennesseans moved to the cities. Young people left the farms where they had grown up and

Both men and women worked in Tennessee factories during World War II.

took jobs in textile mills and other factories. By 1950, Tennessee had shifted from being a predominantly rural state to one that was 55 percent urban. Life was changing in ways no one could have imagined fifty years before.

Generations of African-Americans had lived under the cruel restrictions of the Jim Crow Laws. In the late 1940s and 1950s, black Tennesseans began to push for change. They received crucial support in 1954 when the U.S. Supreme Court ruled that separate schools for black and white children were, by their very nature, unequal. The court ordered that American schools become integrated as soon as possible. The Oak Ridge schools desegregated smoothly in 1956. But violence erupted when black teens enrolled at the all-white high school in nearby Clinton. Enraged white protesters bombed the school, which burned to the ground.

A white employee trying to prevent African-Americans from sitting at a Memphis lunch counter in 1961

While Tennesseans struggled with school desegregation, black college students turned their attention to other arenas. In 1960, student demonstrators organized nonviolent sit-ins at segregated lunch counters in Nashville. The students sat peacefully at the counters, refusing to move until they were served along with white customers. At times, they endured threats and curses. Their firm, gentle approach

Fighting without Bloodshed

Born in Chicago, Diane J. Nash (1938–) arrived in Nashville in 1959 to study at Fisk University. Nash was shocked by the segregated conditions she encountered. She attended a series of workshops on nonviolent protest, which she believed was the most effective way to bring about social change. With the help of other civil-rights activists, she organized sit-in protests at Nashville lunch counters in 1960. Later she helped to organize the "freedom rides" in which blacks and whites rode together on buses through the rigidly segregated states of Mississippi and Alabama. During the late 1960s, Nash was active in protests against the war in Vietnam. She has also been involved in the women's movement. ■

won national respect, and eventually the hated Jim Crow rules crumbled away.

During the 1950s and 1960s, the movement for African-American civil rights transformed the southern states. No black leader had a more powerful impact than Dr. Martin Luther King Jr. (1929–1968), an eloquent Baptist minister from Atlanta, Georgia. Dr. King's Southern Christian Leadership Conference (SCLC) spearheaded nonviolent protests throughout the South. King pushed for racial equality on buses, in schools and universities, in public accommodations, and in the workplace. He was beloved by Americans of all races as an inspired leader and a man of peace.

In April 1968, Dr. King traveled to Memphis to support striking sanitation workers. On the evening of April 4, King stepped onto the balcony of his room at the Lorraine Motel. A shot rang out from across the street, and King fell, mortally wounded. An escaped convict named James Earl Ray was charged with the crime. Ray was found guilty of King's murder and died in prison in 1998.

Healing the Wound

Outraged and grieving over Dr. King's murder, African-Americans rioted in many cities across the United States. King's death left the nation with a terrible psychic wound. To honor Dr. King and to aid the country's healing process, the Lorraine Motel (above) was converted into the National Civil Rights Museum. Opened in 1991, the museum traces the civil rights movement in America. Visitors can stand on King's balcony and gaze into his room, Room 306. With its unmade bed and the remains of breakfast, the room looks much as it did on the fateful morning that Dr. King died. ■

In the final decades of the twentieth century, Tennessee grew and prospered. Corporations opened new industrial plants in the state, lured by its natural and human resources. Nashville achieved leadership in the recording industry. Visitors flocked to Tennessee's parks and other recreation areas. No longer was Tennessee a remote frontier, isolated behind a mountain barricade. It was part of mainstream America at last.

CHAPTER FIVE

Three States in One

"Crops and barns lie below them [the farms]; above are pasture fields, below or around is the orchard with beehives. Each thing is suited to its particular location. Such a farm has a quality unknown in any other for it feels the changing shape of hill shadow; the winter afternoons when all below lies cold and blue and the creek pools slowly skim with ice, the upper slopes are warm and bright; or on another farm the child coming home from school on the southern side of a hill steps from a snowless world of sunshine into a snowy waste of limestone crag and undripping icicles that lie above his northwardly sloping home."

—Novelist Harriette Arnow, describing farms in
Tennessee's Cumberland Valley

Sunrise over the Great Smoky Mountains

Opposite: Fall Creek Falls State Park

The Three Tennessees

Tennessee is a long, narrow state that stretches 482 miles (776 km) from the Mississippi River in the west to the Appalachian Mountains at its eastern tip. It lies in the region sometimes known as the Upper South, just above the Deep South states of Mississippi and Alabama. In area, Tennessee covers 42,146 square miles (109,158 square kilometers), ranking thirty-fourth in total land area among the fifty states.

In the north, Tennessee shares borders with Kentucky and Virginia. North Carolina lies to the east, and Georgia, Alabama, and Mississippi to the south. To the west, across the Mississippi River, Tennessee borders Arkansas and Missouri. Thus eight states hug Tennessee. Missouri is the only other state that shares borders with so many neighbors.

Tennessee's topography

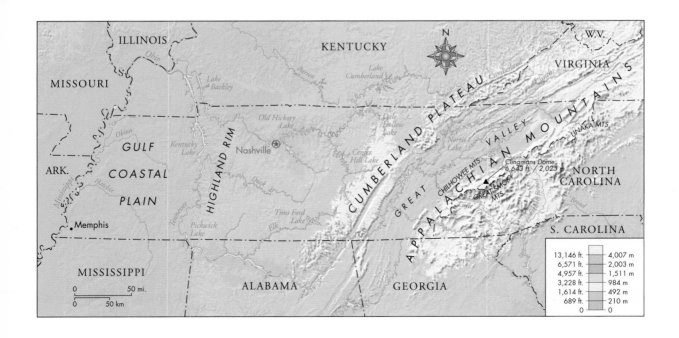

The Golden Shekels

"When the park becomes a reality, millions will annually come through our gates and scatter the golden shekels in our midst," wrote a Knoxville businessman in 1923. He was working on behalf of the campaign to create the Great Smoky Mountains National Park in east Tennessee and western Carolina. President Calvin Coolidge authorized the creation of the park in 1926, but Tennessee and North Carolina had to purchase the necessary land from several powerful timber companies. A series of fierce court battles ensued, dragging over fourteen years. The park finally opened to the public in 1940.

Great Smoky Mountains National Park covers more than 521,000 acres (211,005 ha) of land, about half in North Carolina and half in Tennessee. It preserves some of the most scenic areas in eastern North America, with meadows, streams, waterfalls, and old-growth forests. Because it lies within a day's drive of Washington, D.C., Philadelphia, New York, and other large cities, it is the most frequently visited national park in the United States. Nearly 9 million visitors pass through the park each year, pouring approximately $700 million into the North Carolina and Tennessee economies. Just as park supporters promised in 1923, the "golden shekels" are rolling in. ■

If you meet a native of the Volunteer State, chances are he will not introduce himself by saying that he comes from Tennessee. Instead he will say, "I'm from east Tennessee," or "I grew up in middle Tennessee," or perhaps, "I'm from west Tennessee, on the Delta." Tennessee's unique arrangement of rivers, mountains, and lowlands breaks the state into three distinct sections. Each section has its own resources and its own individual character.

A region of jagged mountains, east Tennessee is the highest part of the state. On average, the altitude is 5,000 feet (1,525 m) above sea level. These mountains were created by great upheavals of Earth millions of years ago. At one time, these mountains were probably as high as the Himalaya of Nepal.

A Path through the Mountains

Until the mid-1700s, the Appalachian Mountains divided Tennessee from the British colonies to the east. Then, in the 1750s, long hunters found a route through the mountains that the Cherokee and other Indians had been using for centuries. This high pass, called the Cumberland Gap, crosses the mountains where Virginia, Tennessee, and Kentucky meet. The Cumberland Gap proved a reliable route for colonists who wished to trade or settle on the western frontier. The famous pioneer Daniel Boone (1734–1820) led many parties of settlers through the Cumberland Gap into Kentucky. Boone helped clear the Wilderness Road, an important trail through the Gap.

Today, visitors can follow in the footsteps of the early settlers at Cumberland Gap National Historical Park. Opened in 1959, this 22,000-acre (8,910-ha) park lies within the borders of Virginia, Kentucky, and Tennessee. The Wilderness Road has been restored to look much as it did during Daniel Boone's lifetime. Twin tunnels (above), completed in 1996, carry automobile traffic through the Gap. ■

East Tennessee's ranges belong to the great Appalachian mountain chain that extends from New England to Georgia and Alabama. Appalachian ranges in east Tennessee include the Chilhowees, Snowbirds, Unakas, and Great Smokies. Clingmans Dome, the highest point in the state at 6,643 feet (2,026 m), stands in Great Smoky Mountains National Park.

The mountainous landscape of east Tennessee is stippled with deep, half-hidden valleys called hollows. A wide, fertile valley called the Great Valley slants across east Tennessee from Virginia into Georgia. East Tennessee also includes the high, fertile Cumberland Plateau with its rich deposits of coal, oil, and natural gas.

Middle Tennessee resembles a deep bowl, its rim composed of steep mountain slopes. The Highland Rim, as it is called, is honeycombed with caves and underground streams. Within the Highland Rim lies the Nashville Basin, sprawling over 6,450 square miles (16,706 sq km). This low, relatively level region is noted for its exceptional grazing land.

West Tennessee belongs to a geographical region known as the Gulf Coastal Plain. The Gulf Coastal Plain stretches northward along the Mississippi River all the way from the Gulf of Mexico to southern Illinois. Most of this region consists of low, rolling hills and streams. High scenic bluffs flank the Mississippi south of Memphis. North of Memphis lies a low, fertile plain commonly referred to as the Delta. Its soil is enriched by silt that washes down the Mississippi.

Just as they vary in scenery, the three regions of Tennessee differ in climate. West Tennessee is the warmest, most humid portion of the state. Winters are relatively mild, with January temperatures

Exploring the Depths

Southeast of the town of McMinnville lies the entrance to the Cumberland Caverns, one of the most extensive cave systems in the United States. During the Civil War, the caves were mined for saltpeter, a mineral used in the manufacture of gunpowder. Picks, shovels, and other mining equipment can still be seen in some passageways. The largest room in the caves is the Hall of the Mountain King. Visitors can tour many parts of the cave system, crawling through holes and sloshing through pools 18 inches (46 cm) deep before they see daylight again. ■

**Cattle grazing
on rich Tennessee
farmland**

Tennessee's Geographical Features

Total area; rank	42,146 sq. mi. (109,158 sq km); 36th
Land; rank	41,220 sq. mi. (106,760 sq km); 34th
Water; rank	926 sq. mi. (2,398 sq km); 30th
Inland water; **rank**	926 sq. mi. (2,398 sq km); 24th
Geographic center	Rutherford County, 5 miles (8 km) northeast of Murfreesboro
Highest point	Clingmans Dome, 6,643 feet (2,026 m)
Lowest point	In Shelby County, 182 feet (56 m)
Largest city	Memphis
Population; rank	4,896,641 (1990 census); 17th
Record high temperature	113°F (45°C) at Perryville on July 29, 1930, and August 9, 1930
Record low temperature	−32°F (−36°C) at Mountain View on December 30, 1917
Average July temperature	78°F (26°C)
Average January temperature	38°F (3°C)
Average annual precipitation	52 inches (132 cm)

averaging 40° Fahrenheit (4° Celsius). Summers have a steamy, subtropical flavor. In July, temperatures average 79°F (26°C). In contrast, east Tennessee has an average January temperature of 37°F (3°C) and July temperatures averaging 71°F (22°C).

Though Tennessee's climate is generally mild, it is sometimes subject to extremes. On December 30, 1917, the mercury plunged to a bone-chilling −32°F (−36°C) at Mountain View, setting the state's all-time low-temperature record. During the summer of 1930, Perryville twice reached the record-breaking high of 113°F (45°C), on July 29 and again on August 9.

Severe blizzards rarely hit Tennessee, but some snow falls every year. West Tennessee receives about 5 inches (13 centimeters) of snow, and east Tennesseans can expect twice as much. The average annual precipitation in the state—a combination of rain, snow, and sleet—is 52 inches (132 cm). Heavy rains often fall in March and April, causing rivers to overflow their banks.

Water, Water Everywhere!

If a time traveler from 1910 were to walk the banks of the Tennessee River today, she would not guess where she was. She would never believe this long series of dams and reservoirs is the wild, often treacherous river she once knew. Since the 1930s, the Tennessee Valley Authority (TVA) has dammed and bulldozed all along the course of the Tennessee and its tributaries. It has built locks and bridges. It has flooded pastures to create reservoirs, and drained marshes to create farmland. Human hands have worked with the river like the hands of a sculptor shaping clay.

Some people feel the efforts of the TVA have had a disastrous impact on the environment, destroying the habitats of countless plants and animals. The TVA has redesigned Tennessee's river systems in an effort to better serve human needs. Whether its work is for good or ill will be debated for decades to come.

The shape of the Tennessee River has given rise to one of Tennessee's nicknames, the Big Bend State. The Tennessee rises in the Appalachian Mountains of east Tennessee and flows south into Alabama. There it bends, flowing west and north until it enters Tennessee again near Shiloh National Military Park. It continues north through Kentucky until it joins the Ohio River. On a map, it appears that there are two Tennessee Rivers coursing through Tennessee, one in the east and the other in the west.

Because of the work of the TVA, barges navigate the Tennessee for its entire length of 650 miles (1,046 km). TVA dams also control most of the Tennessee's tributaries. Among these tributaries are the Clinch, Big Sandy, Duck, French Broad, Elk, Powell, Sequatchie, and Little Tennessee. The Tennessee-Tombigbee

The twists and turns of
the Tennessee River

Waterway is a channel built to connect the Tennessee with the
Tombigbee River in Alabama and Mississippi. Ships on the Tennessee now have direct access to the Gulf of Mexico.

Like the Tennessee River, the Cumberland rises in east Tennessee's mountains. The Cumberland and its branches have also
been dammed and restructured by the TVA. Branches of the Cumberland River include the Caney, Harpeth, and Stones.

The rivers in west Tennessee flow directly into the Mississippi.
Among these Mississippi tributaries are the Hatchie, Forked Deer,
Obion, Wolf, and Loosahatchie.

The TVA has created so many lakes and reservoirs in east and
middle Tennessee that Tennessee now has twice as much inland

Legacy of Violence

Beautiful Reelfoot Lake in northwest Tennessee was formed in 1811 and 1812 by a series of spectacular earthquakes. The New Madrid Quakes, as these upheavals are called, shifted the bed of the Mississippi River and formed a deep depression that filled with water. In 1908, the Tennessee Land Company, a private corporation, launched plans to drain portions of the lake to create tobacco plantations. Residents who hunted and fished in the area for food were outraged. A group of local men known as the Night Riders of Reelfoot kidnapped two company officers, one of whom was murdered. Eventually the state of Tennessee settled the dispute by purchasing the lake and creating Reelfoot Lake State Resort Park (above). ■

water as it had in 1933 when TVA operations began. Among Tennessee's artificial lakes are Boone, Cherokee, Chickamauga, Norris, Fort Loudoun, and Fort Patrick Henry Reservoirs. Kentucky Lake is the biggest human-made lake in the state. Reelfoot Lake is the only large natural lake in Tennessee.

Woods, Fields, and Streams

Tennessee's natural beauty is one of its finest resources. The state's woods and streams can be enjoyed in fifty-one state parks and thirteen state forests, as well as in the magnificent Great Smoky Mountains National Park. In all, forests cover more than half of Tennessee's land area. These forests include more than 13 million acres (5.3 million ha) that can be harvested as commercial timber.

Not surprisingly, plant life varies from one region to another. Evergreens, including hemlock, spruce, pine, and southern balsam, grow on the mountain slopes of east Tennessee. Hardwood trees include maples, several species of oak, cherry, and yellow poplar. Cedars grow along the ridges of the Highland Rim in middle Tennessee, while sweet gum, willow, sycamore, and scrub oak thrive in the Nashville Basin. Trees on the moist, fertile lowlands of west Tennessee are more typically seen in the Deep South—pecan, swamp locust, tupelo, catalpa, and cypress.

Autumn color along the Little Pigeon River

A Second Chance

In the late 1960s, scientists mourned the passing of the Tennessee coneflower, a wildflower native to the Nashville Basin. No specimens had been found in years, and it seemed that the plant was extinct. But, in 1973, a few clusters were discovered at Stones River National Battlefield. Today, this delicate plant (left), with its lovely pale purple blossoms, is protected as a threatened species and getting a second chance at survival. ■

Wildflowers brighten woods and fields throughout Tennessee. In early spring, saxifrage, hepaticas, and bloodroot peek from among fallen leaves and twigs. Wild honeysuckle adds its fragrance to summer evenings. Daisies, black-eyed Susans, wild asters, gentians, and violets blossom in late summer and early fall. Ginseng and goldenseal, which grow in the mountains, are

Tennessee's parks and forests

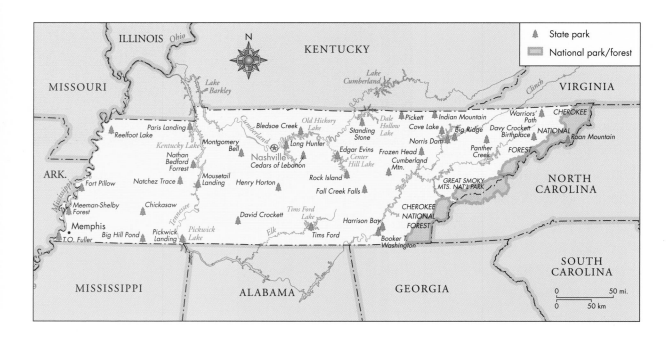

gathered and sold for medicinal purposes. The trillium, or wake robin, is a cherished flower of the Great Smokies. A distinctive crimson V marks the base of its petals.

When the long hunters came to Tennessee in the 1700s, they found a wealth of game—elk, deer, and even bison. Within a few decades, the elk and bison disappeared, wiped out by excessive hunting. Today white-tailed deer are still plentiful in most parts of Tennessee. Some black bears are found in the mountains. Red foxes, gray foxes, opossums, skunks, mink, flying squirrels, and muskrats live throughout the state. Wild hogs called razorbacks wallow in the swamps and marshes. The ancestors of these pigs escaped from farms and learned to forage for roots, berries, and other food.

More than 300 bird species can be found in Tennessee, including many that migrate through the state in spring and fall. An active nesting colony of bald eagles lives around Reelfoot Lake. Herons and egrets nest in the trees along the Cumberland, Tennessee, and other rivers. Rare golden eagles can be spotted in the Smokies while the gobbling of wild turkeys is heard in remote parts of the eastern mountains. In spring, the woods ring with the notes of such songbirds as the robin, mockingbird, eastern towhee, and Carolina wren.

Tennessee's rivers and reservoirs offer exceptional fishing. Brook trout, catfish, and large- and small-mouth bass are native to the state. The highly prized rainbow trout was introduced to Tennessee streams from rivers in the western United States.

Sometimes golden eagles are seen in Tennessee.

CHAPTER SIX

Turns in the Road

Through much of Tennessee, the roads and highways twist among mountains and hollows. The views can be spectacular as you reach the top of a ridge and gaze at the wooded hills and valleys around you. The roads link Tennessee's towns and cities to one another and open them to visitors who want to explore the state.

The Rocky Mount Historical Site

East Tennessee

The rugged mountains of east Tennessee were a challenge to the early settlers. Nevertheless, many important cities and fascinating small towns managed to take root in this beautiful region.

Bristol is one of the few towns in the nation that is shared between two states. The Tennessee–Virginia line runs down the middle of one of Bristol's main streets. Indians used the nearby Bristol Caverns as hiding places during battles with white settlers. Today the caverns are among Bristol's leading attractions. Bristol also takes pride in the South Holston Dam, one of the more unusual creations of the TVA. Built of soil rather than concrete, South Holston is the third-largest earthen dam in the world.

Home to East Tennessee State University, Johnson City is a small town with a rich cultural life. The Carroll Reece Museum on the university campus hosts many traveling art and historical

Opposite: A road leading through some of Tennessee's mountains

exhibits. The museum's permanent collections include toys, musical instruments, and furniture from Tennessee's pioneer era. Visitors get a vivid glimpse of pioneer life at Rocky Mount, once the home of Tennessee's territorial governor, William Blount. Rocky Mount is a living-history museum where guides in period costumes act the roles of Blount and his acquaintances.

Jonesborough was founded in 1780, making it the oldest town in Tennessee. For four years, Jonesborough served as capital of the "Lost State of Franklin." The downtown area is graced with many

Tell Me a Story!

It is sometimes said that everyone has a story to tell. The adage proves true on a three-day weekend each October as people stream into Jonesborough from all over the country.

Since 1973, Jonesborough has been the setting for the National Storytelling Festival. People of all ages gather to spin yarns of every variety (above). Some tell hilarious tall tales, some tell stories of daring adventure and, as darkness falls, some tell ghost stories that will give you delicious shivers. ■

fine old houses, some built before 1800. Widely thought to be the oldest log cabin in Tennessee, the Christopher Taylor House stands on Main Street. Behind the Jonesborough Visitors' Center and Museum is Duncan's Meadow, where General Andrew Jackson once fought a duel.

In 1982, the Knoxville World's Fair transformed the city. World's Fair Park was created in the valley of Second Creek. Today the most striking reminder of the fair is the Sunsphere, a unique twenty-six-story tower. The top five stories are a giant globe with an observation deck that offers visitors a magnificent view of the city.

Sunsphere was created for the 1982 World's Fair.

During the 1990s, Knoxville revitalized its downtown area with the construction of Volunteer Landing, a 1-mile (1.6-km)-long riverfront walkway lined with attractive shops and restaurants. Just off the river walk is the James White Fort, a log structure dating to 1786. The fort was moved to Knoxville in 1968 and includes a smokehouse, blacksmith shop, and other outbuildings. The Museum of East Tennessee History has fascinating exhibits on frontier life, the Civil War, and the development of the Tennessee

River. Among its most prized exhibits are a gun that once belonged to Davy Crockett and the marriage license issued to Crockett in 1809.

Another intriguing Knoxville museum is the Beck Cultural Center, which traces the history of African-Americans in the Knoxville area. The Frank H. McClung Museum, on the University of Tennessee campus, displays east Tennessee minerals, Indian artifacts, and historical items.

A nineteenth-century preacher from the tiny town of Black Oak Ridge predicted that an important city would someday spring up in the region. "Thousands of people will be running to and fro," he wrote. "They will be making things and there will be a great noise and confusion and the world will shake." In 1942, this strange prediction came true when the U.S. government created Oak Ridge, Tennessee, as a secret research station to develop the world's first atomic weapons. Today, Oak Ridge is a highly cultured community, home to many scientists and engineers who work at Oak Ridge National Laboratory. The Oak Ridge Children's Museum has a remarkable array of hands-on activities that teach the basics of physics and chemistry.

On Market Street in downtown Chattanooga stands a great domed building known as the Chattanooga Choo-choo, formerly the terminal of the

The Chattanooga Choo-choo is now a historical landmark.

Southern Railway. The name is a tribute to an old song that once made the Chattanooga Choo-choo a household word. Today the "choo-choo" is an arcade of shops, restaurants, and hotels. Chattanooga celebrates its history in Ross's Landing Park and Plaza. Statues in the park commemorate Sequoyah, who invented the Cherokee writing system; Bessie Smith, the African-American blues singer; and many others. The Tennessee Aquarium offers a unique view of life in a North American river. Exhibits show the plants and animals that live in various parts of a river, from the first trickling stream at its source to the brackish mouth where it reaches the sea. Creatures of a more fanciful kind are on view at the Dragon Dreams Museum, an eight-room house filled with dragons great and small from all over the world.

Middle Tennessee

Much of middle Tennessee is a rolling plateau of fertile farmland. Cattle and horses graze in fields along the roads. Nashville, the state capital, is the centerpiece of this region. But middle Tennessee also has many fascinating smaller towns and cities.

Fifteen square blocks of downtown Franklin have been listed on the National Register of Historic Places. The town center is a charming tree-lined square. Franklin preserves dozens of stately homes from the antebellum, or pre-Civil War, period. One of the most interesting is Carter House, built in 1831. Union troops used Carter House as their headquarters during the Battle of Franklin. One of the Carter sons, Tod, died of wounds he received in the battle that raged within sight of his own home.

Murfreesboro was Tennessee's state capital from 1818 to

Lookout Mountain

One of Chattanooga's most popular features is Lookout Mountain, a few miles southwest of the city. Among the mountain's attractions is Ruby Falls (above), a 145-foot (44-m) waterfall within a limestone cave. The effect of the falls is heightened by music and a light show. Visitors to the Lookout Mountain Battlefield can walk in the footsteps of Union and Confederate soldiers who fought the Battle above the Clouds in November 1863. ■

Carter House is one of the many historical homes in Franklin.

1826. The town was called Cannonsburgh before the Revolutionary War. The Pioneer Village of Cannonsburgh re-creates life on the middle Tennessee frontier with log cabins, a one-room schoolhouse, a gristmill, and other reconstructed buildings. As a study in contrast, another part of the village recalls Murfreesboro in 1925 with a vintage doctor's office, car-repair garage, and many more surprises. For a glimpse of plantation life

Tennessee's cities and interstates

Jackson's Hermitage

About 15 miles (24 km) east of Nashville stands the Hermitage, once the stately home of Andrew Jackson and his family. Jackson bought the land in 1804 and began building the Hermitage in 1819. He is buried in the garden beside his beloved wife, Rachel, who died before he took office. The state of Tennessee has maintained the Hermitage as a historic site since 1888. Many of the furnishings on view belonged to Jackson. ■

before the Civil War, visitors may tour Oaklands, the home of the Maney family. Twelve rooms have been fully restored with authentic period furniture.

Manchester was founded as a cotton-mill town, using the Duck River to power the machinery. Today, Manchester has a pleasant small-town atmosphere. A main attraction is the combined Museum Arrowheads and Aerospace Cultural Center. It has an unusual variety of exhibits including minerals, Indian artifacts, military weapons, quilts, and antique dolls. Outside Manchester, 82 acres (33 ha) of tallgrass prairie are carefully preserved by the federal government as a National Natural Landmark. During the summer, prairie grasses may stand 12 feet (4 m) high.

Nashville, the capital of Tennessee since 1826, has long been a thriving cultural center. In the nineteenth century, it was nicknamed "the Athens of the South" after the glorious capital of ancient Greece. In honor of its namesake, Nashville erected a replica of the splendid Greek temple, the Parthenon, for Tennessee's 1896 Centennial Exposition. Nashville's Parthenon is the world's only full-sized replica of the original Athenian structure. Inside is a 42-foot (13-m) statue of Athena, the ancient Greek goddess of wisdom, said to be the largest indoor sculpture in the world.

Nashville is the capital of Tennessee.

During the 1990s, Nashville renovated a stretch of decaying property along the Cumberland River. The District, as this area is called, has a lively array of shops, restaurants, and nightclubs.

Besides being the capital of Tennessee, Nashville is known the world over as the capital of the country-music industry. The section of town called Music Row holds the offices of some of country music's biggest recording companies. The Country Music Hall of Fame and Museum boasts an extravagant collection of memorabilia—costumes, sheet music, photos, and videos. Fans love to visit the museum's Studio B, where such greats as Elvis Presley, Roy Orbison, and Dolly Parton recorded hit albums. Nearby is another popular stop for tourists, the Car Collectors Hall of Fame. Among its exhibits are a Cadillac Eldorado that once belonged to Elvis Presley and a 1982 Buick Riviera custom-built for country singer Tammy Wynette.

West Tennessee

The western bend of the Tennessee River serves as the boundary between middle and west Tennessee. In character, west Tennessee is more southern than any other part of the state. Before the Civil War, it was a region of large plantations. The Mississippi River is a major force that shapes the towns along its banks.

The town of Jackson grew up along the railroad between Nashville and Memphis, so it is not surprising that Jackson has two railroad museums. The South Royal Depot is a fully restored 1907 station filled with mementos from Jackson's railway past. The Casey Jones Home and Railroad Museum celebrates the legend of America's most famous train engineer. On display are such items

Round and Round We Go!

One of the world's most unusual merry-go-rounds is the Foxtrot Carousel in Nashville's Riverfront Park. Red Grooms, an artist who was born in Nashville but went on to make his fortune in New York, designed the carousel. Instead of horses, Grooms designed thirty-six figures of famous Tennesseans, including Andrew Jackson and Olympic athlete Wilma Rudolph. ■

The Casey Jones Home and Railroad Museum

The Ballad of Casey Jones

"I'm gonna run her till she leaves the rail,/ Or make it on time with the southbound mail." According to the famous ballad by Wallace Saunders, the fireman on Jones's train, those were the engineer's final words. John Luther "Casey" Jones (1864–1900) died in a train wreck in Mississippi, but his heroic actions saved his passengers and crew. Jones grew up in Kentucky, but he lived in Jackson, Tennessee, during his later years. ■

as Jones's watch and the hearse that carried his body after the crash in which he died.

Brownsville, in the heart of the Tennessee Delta, is the seat of Haywood County. Before the Civil War, Haywood had more slaves than any other county in the state. Today, Brownsville is home to the Felsenthal Lincoln Collection, a museum crammed with lithographs, documents, and other mementos of the president who freed the slaves. Brownsville is chiefly known as a center of country blues, a heartfelt music created by black singers early in the twentieth century. Blues artists from the Brownsville area are honored at the Music Museum of the Tennessee Delta Heritage Center. The center also includes the Hatchie River Ecosystem Museum and the Cotton Museum.

Nashville is to ancient Greece what Memphis was to ancient Egypt. In keeping with this theme, Memphis Pyramid Arena, a 22,500-seat sports stadium, was designed to look like the pyramid of an Egyptian pharaoh. A statue of the great Pharaoh Ramses, cast from the Egyptian original, guards the entrance.

Memphis is a busy port city.

The Pyramid Arena is a large sports stadium.

Memphis was born and grew up as a river port. Its reverence for the river is apparent in the River Walk at Mud Island. The River Walk is a detailed scale model representing 900 miles (1,448 km) of the Mississippi's course, from Cairo, Illinois, to the Gulf of Mexico. The waters of this artificial river stretch for five blocks, at a scale of 30 inches (76 cm) to 1 mile (1.6 km). The Gulf is represented by a large public swimming pool. The Mud Island complex includes the Mud Island Amphitheater and the Mississippi River Museum.

The history of Memphis comes alive in several beautifully restored historic houses. Among them is the red-brick Hunt–Phelan Home, built by slaves between 1828 and 1832. During the Civil War, when

Union troops occupied Tennessee, this house served as headquarters for General Ulysses S. Grant. The Slavehaven–Burkle Estate Museum was once a stop on the Underground Railroad, which helped runaway slaves escape to freedom. Guides are happy to show the workings of the house's trapdoors and secret tunnels.

To lovers of blues music, Memphis is the most special spot on Earth. It was here, on Beale Street, that the masters of this musical form truly found their voice. Today, devotees make their pilgrimage to Beale Street to visit the homes of such blues greats as W. C. Handy and B. B. King. The Center of Southern Folklore provides tours of Beale Street and hosts evening blues concerts.

The Slavehaven–Burkle Estate Museum

Graceland

Elvis Presley's Memphis mansion, Graceland (right), is the second-most-visited house in America. Only the White House receives more tourists. Elvis lived at Graceland for twenty years, from 1957 until his death. Presley fans can gaze at the star's gold-plated automobiles and his two personal jet planes, and walk in reverence through his Hall of Gold Records. A favorite room houses the Sincerely Collection, displaying Elvis's personal record library, his sneakers, and gifts from his fans. Among them is a plaque made entirely from chewing-gum wrappers. All Graceland tours end at Presley's grave in the Meditation Garden. Entrance to the garden is free of charge early each morning, and hundreds come at dawn to pay their respects to the man who helped make rock and roll. ■

To millions of people around the world, Memphis means only one name, and only one name means Memphis—Elvis Presley. Elvis Presley (1935–1977), "the King" to his adoring fans, recorded his first hit songs at Sun Studio in Memphis in 1954. Visitors to this small, unpretentious studio may touch the very microphone that once captured Elvis's crooning voice.

CHAPTER SEVEN

From a Hilltop in Nashville

The Tennessee state capitol has a fascinating history. William Strickland, the architect who designed the building, included his own tomb in the blueprint. He died while construction was still underway and is buried underneath the capitol's northeast corner.

During the Civil War, the capitol served as headquarters for Andrew Johnson, Tennessee's military governor. Built of Tennessee limestone, this lovely building gazes down upon Nashville from the highest hill in the city. It is the seat of state government and a proud reminder of Tennessee's long and dramatic history.

Of the People, For the People

Tennessee has operated under its present constitution since 1870. The state had two earlier constitutions, the first approved in 1796 and the second in 1834. The constitution divides the state government into three branches, much like the branches of the federal

The General Assembly is made up of the senate and the house of representatives.

Opposite: The state capitol

Tennessee's Governors

Name	Party	Term	Name	Party	Term
John Sevier	Dem.-Rep.	1796–1801	John P. Buchanan	Dem.	1891–1893
Archibald Roane	Dem.-Rep.	1801–1803	Peter Turney	Dem.	1893–1897
John Sevier	Dem.-Rep.	1803–1809	Robert Love Taylor	Dem.	1897–1899
Willie Blount	Dem.-Rep.	1809–1815	Benton McMillin	Dem.	1899–1903
Joseph McMinn	Dem.-Rep.	1815–1821	James B. Frazier	Dem.	1903–1905
William Carroll	Dem.-Rep.	1821–1827	John I. Cox	Dem.	1905–1907
Sam Houston	Dem.-Rep.	1827–1829	Malcolm R. Patterson	Dem.	1907–1911
William Hall	Dem.	1829	Ben W. Hooper	Rep.	1911–1915
William Carroll	Dem.	1829–1835	Tom C. Rye	Dem.	1915–1919
Newton Cannon	Whig	1835–1839	A. H. Roberts	Dem.	1919–1921
James K. Polk	Dem.	1839–1841	Alfred A. Taylor	Rep.	1921–1923
James C. Jones	Whig	1841–1845	Austin Peay	Dem.	1923–1927
Aaron V. Brown	Dem.	1845–1847	Henry H. Horton	Dem.	1927–1933
Neill S. Brown	Whig	1847–1849	Hill McAlister	Dem.	1933–1937
William Trousdale	Dem.	1849–1851	Gordon Browning	Dem.	1937–1939
William B. Campbell	Whig	1851–1853	Prentice Cooper	Dem.	1939–1945
Andrew Johnson	Dem.	1853–1857	Jim McCord	Dem.	1945–1949
Isham G. Harris	Dem.	1857–1862	Gordon Browning	Dem.	1949–1953
Andrew Johnson (Military governor)	Dem.	1862–1865	Frank G. Clement	Dem.	1953–1959
			Buford Ellington	Dem.	1959–1963
William G. Brownlow	Whig-Rep.	1865–1869	Frank G. Clement	Dem.	1963–1967
DeWitt Clinton Senter	Whig-Rep.	1869–1871	Buford Ellington	Dem.	1967–1971
John C. Brown	Whig-Dem.	1871–1875	Winfield Dunn	Rep.	1971–1975
James D. Porter	Dem.	1875–1879	Leonard Ray Blanton	Dem.	1975–1979
Albert S. Marks	Dem.	1879–1881	Lamar Alexander	Rep.	1979–1987
Alvin Hawkins	Rep.	1881–1883	Ned McWherter	Dem.	1987–1995
William B. Bate	Dem.	1883–1887	Don Sundquist	Rep.	1995–
Robert Love Taylor	Dem.	1887–1891			

government in Washington, D.C. The legislative branch passes and repeals laws. The judicial branch, or court system, interprets the laws. The executive branch, or office of the governor, sees that the laws are carried out.

The governor, or chief executive, may serve any number of four-year terms in the course of a lifetime. But only two terms can be consecutive. Next in line below the governor is the lieutenant governor, who also serves as speaker of the senate. The governor appoints the heads of twenty-one state-run agencies.

Tennessee's general assembly is divided into two houses. The upper house, or senate, has thirty-three members who are elected to four-year terms. Ninety-nine members are elected to serve two-year terms in the lower house, or house of representatives. The legislature appoints the secretary of state, the state treasurer, and the comptroller of the state treasury.

Tennessee's counties

Governor Don Sundquist

Regular sessions of the general assembly are held in odd-numbered years and may not exceed ninety days. A special session can be called at any time by the governor or by a vote of two-thirds of the members of each house.

The judicial system of Tennessee resembles a vast pyramid. Municipal and county courts form the pyramid's base, along with specialized courts dealing with juveniles and domestic relations. At the next level, the state is divided into thirty-one districts served by circuit courts. Above the circuit courts are the appellate courts. At the peak of the pyramid is Tennessee's state supreme court with one chief justice and four associate justices. Thus a case may be filed in a county court, tried in a circuit court, appealed to one of the appellate courts, and passed on to the supreme court for its final appeal within the state.

Local government in Tennessee operates on the county and municipal levels. Tennessee has ninety-five counties. County com-

The Boss of Memphis

Edward H. Crump (1874–1954) never mastered the art of public speaking. Nevertheless, he was an extraordinary politician who controlled the city of Memphis for more than forty years. Under Crump, the city government ran cheaply and efficiently. But Crump's government was full of corruption, and those who opposed him paid a heavy price. Crump was especially harsh toward labor-union supporters and leaders in the African-American community.

"Boss Crump," as he was called, knew how to get others to do his bidding. He could get out the votes for any candidate of his choice. In 1932, Crump supported the winning candidate for governor, Henry H. Horton. Working behind the scenes, Crump managed to control state government for the next sixteen years. ∎

Tennessee's State Government

Executive Branch

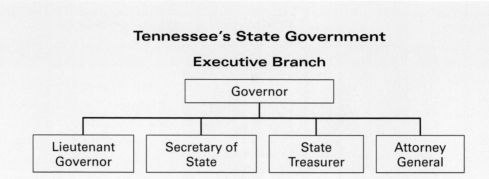

```
                    Governor
        ┌──────────┬────┴─────┬──────────┐
   Lieutenant   Secretary of   State      Attorney
   Governor        State      Treasurer   General
```

Legislative Branch

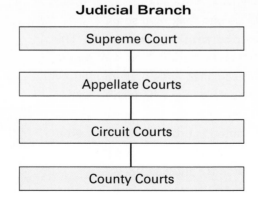

```
            General Assembly
        ┌────────┴────────┐
      Senate      House of Representatives
```

Judicial Branch

Supreme Court

Appellate Courts

Circuit Courts

County Courts

Tennessee's State Symbols

State bird: Mockingbird

About 10 inches (25 cm) in length, this grayish bird (above) is unassuming in appearance. But its strong, beautiful song rings out across Tennessee through the spring and summer months. Mockingbirds are excellent mimics, weaving the calls of many other birds into their own song.

State animal: Raccoon

The "masked bandit," as it is sometimes called, was once hunted by mountain men with baying hound dogs. Today, the raccoon has adapted to urban life and can even twist the lids from garbage cans to search for snacks.

State flower: Iris

The iris (left) is a popular garden flower that comes in many varieties and colors. Irises often have drooping outer petals called falls. The falls of some species are "bearded," or fuzzy to the touch.

State wildflower: Passionflower

Passionflowers grow on a vine that climbs 8 to 20 feet (2.4 to 6 m) high on the trunks of trees. The vine produces edible berries and large flowers of various colors.

State tree: Tulip poplar

Sometimes called the yellow poplar, this graceful shade tree grows in many Tennessee gardens and along city streets. In the spring, it produces long, drooping flowers called catkins.

State gem: Freshwater pearl

Mussels that live in lakes and rivers produce beautiful pearls (below), just as oysters do in the ocean. Some of the world's most valuable freshwater pearls have been found in the Mississippi River and its tributaries.

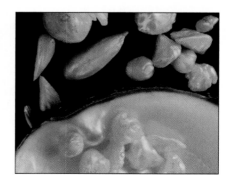

Tennessee's State Song
"My Homeland, Tennessee"

Tennessee lists five official state songs. The oldest of these is
"My Homeland, Tennessee," adopted in 1925.
Words by Nell Grayson Taylor and music by Roy Lamont Smith.

O Tennessee, that gave us birth,
To thee our hearts bow down.
For thee our love and loyalty
Shall weave a fadeless crown.
Thy purple hills our cradle was;
Thy fields our mother breast;
Beneath thy sunny bended skies
Our childhood days were blessed.

Chorus:
O Tennessee, fair Tennessee,
Our love for thee can never die:
Dear homeland, Tennessee.
Twas long ago our fathers came,
A free and noble band,
Across the mountains' frowning
    heights

To seek a promised land.
And here before their raptured
    eyes,
In beauteous majesty:
Outspread the smiling valleys
Of the winding Tennessee.
Could we forget our heritage
Of heroes strong and brave?
Could we do aught but cherish it,
Unsullied to the grave?
Ah no! The state where Jackson
    sleeps
Shall ever peerless be.
We glory in thy majesty;
Our homeland, Tennessee!

missioners from around the state meet four times a year to discuss
their concerns. Altogether, the state of Tennessee has 335 cities and
towns.

Tennessee is one of the few states with no state income tax, so
money is raised in different ways. About half of Tennessee's revenue comes from sales, corporate, and other taxes. The state gets
the rest through a variety of grants and programs sponsored by the
federal government.

Tennessee State Flag and Seal

The state flag of Tennessee has a red background, with a band of blue along the right side separated from the red by a thin line of white. On the red field is a blue circle containing three white stars. The stars represent the state's three sections—east, middle, and west Tennessee. The state flag was adopted in 1905.

The upper half of the state seal bears the word AGRICULTURE. Pictures of a plow, a sheaf of wheat, and a cotton plant represent farming in the state. The lower half of the seal has the word COMMERCE and the image of a riverboat. Around the border of the seal are inscribed the words, "THE GREAT SEAL OF THE STATE OF TENNESSEE, 1796." The state seal came into use in the years after the Civil War but was not officially adopted until 1987. ■

Running for Office

The Republican Party was founded in 1854 to fight for the abolition of slavery. As a slaveholding state, Tennessee reacted by becoming staunchly Democratic. Its allegiance to the Democratic Party continued after the Civil War, when the Republicans were associated with the Reconstruction program. Though the Republicans had a few strongholds in east Tennessee, the Democrats largely controlled the state until the 1960s. In 1966, Howard H.

Born to the Breed

Albert Gore Jr. (1948–) grew up in Washington, D.C., amid the excitement of the nation's political scene. His father, Albert Gore Sr., was a U.S. senator from Tennessee. The younger Gore served in the army after college and spent several years working as a reporter on *The Tennessean,* a Nashville newspaper. In 1976, he was elected to Congress, launching his political career. He served two terms as U.S. vice president under President Bill Clinton, from 1992 to 2000. In August 2000, he was nominated to be the Democratic candidate for president. Throughout his career, Gore has shown a special interest in science, technology, and the environment. ■

Baker Jr. became the first Tennessee Republican elected to a U.S. Senate seat in nearly 100 years.

After the 1960s, Republicans continued to gain ground in Tennessee. By the late 1970s, Tennessee was truly a two-party state. In presidential elections, Democrats have carried Tennessee twice as often as Republican candidates have.

A Man with a Mission

When he was sixteen years old, Cordell Hull (1871–1955) delivered a speech to his class in a middle Tennessee high school. He spoke eloquently on the dangers of protective tariffs in trade. Hull was convinced that the United States and other nations should be able to trade freely with any market throughout the world. Years later, as a U.S. congressman and senator, Hull continued to promote his free-trade philosophy. In 1933, President Franklin D. Roosevelt appointed Hull to serve as secretary of state, a post he held for the next eleven years. After World War II, Hull helped to establish the United Nations. For his contributions to international cooperation, he was honored with the Nobel Prize for Peace in 1945. ■

CHAPTER EIGHT

The Plow
and the
Riverboat

Tennessee's state motto consists of three words: *Agriculture and Commerce*. The motto is represented by images on the state seal. The picture of a riverboat reminds us of Tennessee's place in the world of trade, and a plow symbolizes the work of Tennessee's farmers. The combined strength of agriculture and commerce gives the state a healthy economy.

There are about 89,000 farms in Tennessee.

Living off the Land

Agriculture accounts for only 1 percent of Tennessee's gross state product (GSP)—the total value of goods and services produced in the state. The state has about 89,000 farms.

Farming, like so much else in Tennessee, is determined by region. The fertile soil of west Tennessee is excellent for growing soybeans and cotton. West Tennessee orchards produce rich har-

Opposite: A farm in Lincoln County

Tennessee Walkers

Crowds pour into Shelbyville each August for the Tennessee Walking Horse National Celebration. For ten days, the finest examples of this lovely breed are on display. Developed in the 1830s, the Tennessee walking horse is noted for its gentleness and intelligence. It moves with a smooth, easy gait called the "running walk." Horse lovers claim that the gait is so smooth you can drink a cup of coffee without spilling a drop as you ride on a Tennessee walker's back. The Tennessee walking horse is big business for horse breeders in Middle Tennessee. ■

vests of apples and peaches. Many west Tennessee farmers raise livestock, especially hogs.

The rolling fields of middle Tennessee provide lush grazing land for beef and dairy cattle. Tobacco is the leading crop for farmers in east Tennessee. Poultry is raised throughout the state, as are crops including hay, snap beans, and tomatoes.

One of the state's main
crops is tobacco.

Digging for Black Diamonds

About three-fourths of Tennessee's coal comes from underground mines. Miners sink a deep shaft and drill branching tunnels along veins of coal. Underground mining can be very dangerous. The air in the tunnels is full of coal dust, which can cause black lung disease and death unless proper safety measures are taken. Strip-mining, another method used in east Tennessee, is less dangerous to humans, but it destroys the landscape. Layer by layer, miners remove an entire hillside to get at the veins of coal beneath the surface. In recent years, laws and growing awareness about the environment have required coal companies to replace and replant the land when a strip mine is exhausted. ■

Beneath the soil of Tennessee lies a wealth of valuable minerals. Quarries produce crushed limestone, used for lining roadbeds and manufacturing concrete. Most limestone quarries are in east Tennessee. East Tennessee is also coal country. Coal is sometimes referred to as "black diamonds."

From the Factories

Manufacturing accounts for about 24 percent of the GSP in Tennessee. Factories in the state turn out chemicals, rubber, plastics, and machinery. Chemical products made in Tennessee include paints and soap. Several companies in the state package processed foods such as bread, flour, and cereals. Large flour mills operate near Chattanooga.

Automobile manufacturing is an important industry for Tennessee.

Among Tennessee's leading manufactured goods are automobiles and auto parts. General Motors operates a plant in Spring Hill. During the 1990s, the Japanese auto manufacturer Nissan opened a factory in Smyrna. Other vehicles are also built in Tennessee. Several companies in Nashville make boats and airplane parts. Lawrenceburg is a center for the manufacture of bicycles.

Fried Green Tomatoes

A special southern treat, this side dish is popular in the Volunteer State.

Ingredients:

4 green tomatoes, medium-sized, unripe

1 cup of buttermilk

salt

black pepper

dash of cayenne pepper

peanut oil

1 cup of corn flour

Directions:

Slice tomatoes into fifths about 1/2-inch wide.

Into the buttermilk, add salt, black pepper, and cayenne pepper to taste. Brush the buttermilk onto the tomatoes, then let them marinate for 1/2 hour or more.

Now ask an adult for help with the frying. In a saucepan, cover the bottom 1/4 inch deep with peanut oil, then heat until hot (not smoking). Dunk the tomatoes in the flour, then shake off any excess. Place in pan, then fry each side for approximately two minutes. Dry on a paper towel.

What Tennessee Grows, Manufactures, and Mines

Agriculture	Manufacturing	Mining
Beef cattle	Chemicals	Coal
Cotton	Fabricated metal products	Stone
Hay	Food products	Zinc
Hogs	Machinery	
Milk	Rubber and plastic products	
Soybeans	Transportation equipment	
Tobacco		

In the 1980s and 1990s, Tennessee moved into the world of high technology. Japanese electronics firms opened factories in Memphis, Knoxville, Jackson, and Lebanon. Some have called Tennessee "the Silicon Valley of the South."

Tennessee's natural resources

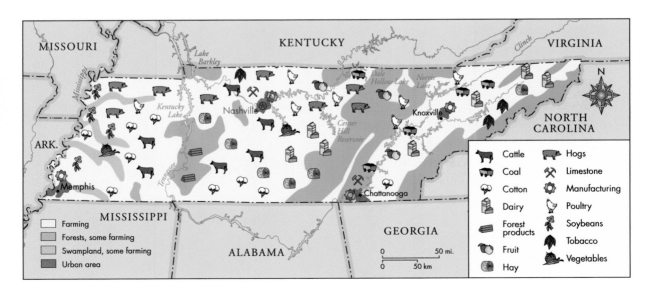

Doing for Others

Tennessee's service industries contribute about 71 percent of the GSP. Service industries are by far the largest sector of the state's economy. People who work in service industries do not produce crops or goods for sale. Instead they provide services to groups or individuals. Teachers, doctors, salesclerks, musicians, real estate salespeople, and bankers are all service-industry workers.

As the state seal suggests, the largest share of the service industries in Tennessee is devoted to wholesale and retail trade. Memphis rose as a major center for the cotton trade early in the

The busy port at Memphis

"When It Absolutely, Positively, Has to Get There Overnight"

In 1973, a young businessman named Frederick Smith launched an unusual new company. He promised the speedy, reliable delivery of letters and packages. Smith's Federal Express Corporation (better known as FedEx) began with offices in an empty hangar at Memphis International Airport. Within ten years, it had grown to be the biggest private delivery company in the world. Federal Express handles about 3 million packages a day, and serves 212 countries. Some 26,000 employees work in and near Memphis. The company headquarters occupy a complex of buildings at the edge of the airport. In a whirlwind of speed, employees weigh, sort, and load packages of all shapes and sizes. Federal Express maintains its own fleet of planes, which take off twenty-four hours a day to ensure that packages arrive on time. ■

nineteenth century. Steamboats plied up and down the Mississippi, loading bales of cotton at the Memphis docks. Today Memphis is still an important center of commerce, followed by Knoxville and Nashville.

Mr. Piggly Wiggly

Early in the twentieth century, most Americans shopped in small stores where clerks served customers from behind a counter. Clarence Saunders (1881–1953) had a different vision. Raised in Palmyra, Tennessee, Saunders worked in the grocery business in Clarksville and Memphis. After careful observation and thought, he designed a store where customers walked through aisles of merchandise, selecting the items they wanted from the shelves. In 1916, Saunders put his ideas into practice when he opened his first Piggly Wiggly store in Memphis. By 1923, some 1,200 Piggly Wigglies had sprung up all over the United States. Despite the store's success, Saunders lost his fortune in the stock market. He is remembered today for popularizing the self-service supermarket and transforming the experience of grocery shopping.

In 1922, Saunders built a magnificent pink marble mansion, which he lost when he went bankrupt the following year. The mansion now houses the Memphis Pink Palace Museum, with extensive exhibits on local animals, birds, and minerals, as well as regional history. One remarkable display is the Clyde Parke Circus, complete with horses, elephants, acrobats, and clowns—all carved from wood and set in motion by intricate machinery. ■

Community, business, and personal services also play a key role in Tennessee's service economy. These services include health care, professional legal services, entertainment, tourism, and hotel accommodations. Finance, insurance, and real estate make up the third-largest portion of the service economy in Tennessee. Government, including the Tennessee Valley Authority, ranks fourth.

A Call for Freedom

One of the best-remembered newspapers in Tennessee history, *The Manumission Intelligencer*, was published for only a few short months. This was the first antislavery, or abolitionist, newspaper in the United States. Its founder, Elihu Embree (1782–1820), was born in Pennsylvania, but he moved to Tennessee and set up a profitable ironworks.

Embree owned slaves as a young man, but when he turned thirty he underwent a change of heart. His newspaper, published in Jonesborough, carried a passionate message to the world. "Freedom," Embree wrote, "is the inalienable right of all men." *The Emancipator* was published until Embree's death from a sudden illness. ■

Making Connections

To function effectively, Tennessee's economy requires reliable systems of transportation and communication. Highway construction began in Tennessee in 1913. Today, the state is threaded with 86,000 miles (138,400 km) of highways and roads. Tennessee is also served by both freight and passenger trains. The busiest airfield is Memphis International Airport, while other commercial airports operate in Knoxville, Nashville, and Chattanooga.

Tennessee's first newspaper was the *Knoxville Gazette*, which went to press in 1791. Leading papers today include the *Tennessean* (Nashville),

Tennessee has 250 radio stations.

the *Commercial Appeal* (Memphis), the *Chattanooga Free Press*, and the *Knoxville News-Sentinel*.

The first radio station in Tennessee, WNAV, went on the air in Knoxville in 1922. WMCT-TV, the first television station in the state, began broadcasting in Memphis in 1948. Today, Tennessee has 250 radio stations, 35 television stations, and 20 cable channels.

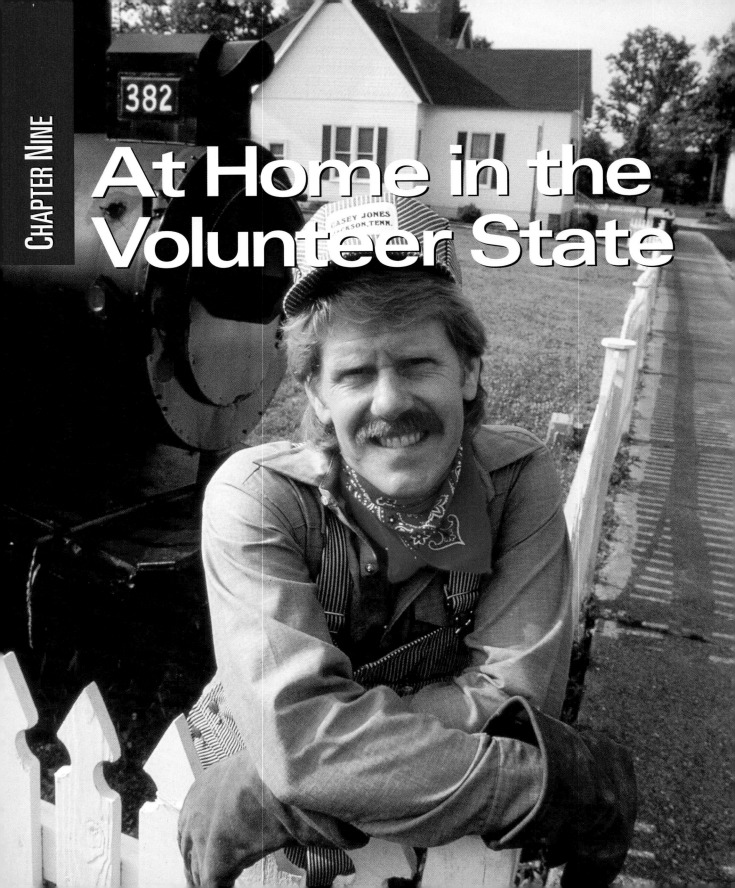

CHAPTER NINE

At Home in the Volunteer State

For four days each October, thousands of people pour into the east Tennessee town of Norris for the Tennessee Fall Homecoming. Sponsored by the Museum of Appalachia, this festival is a celebration of east Tennessee crafts, music, storytelling, and down-home cooking. By day, women and men demonstrate basket making, woodcarving, glassblowing, and pottery making. In the evening, the air is filled with the music of fiddles and banjos, as well as electric drums and guitars. This festival is a rollicking reminder of the traditions that make Tennessee such a special place. Tennesseans cherish their old-time ways, but they also delight in the excitement of modern life. In Tennessee, the old and the new exist comfortably side by side.

Basket making is one of the many crafts Tennessee can be proud of.

People and Places

Population experts predict that Tennessee will have about 5,424,000 people in the year 2000. In 1990, Tennessee had a population of 4,896,641. This means that the state's population jumped 10 percent in the last decade of the twentieth century. Most of this population increase occurred because more and more people are moving to Tennessee from other states and from overseas. Some are

Opposite: At home in rural Tennessee

Knoxville is one of the largest cities in the state.

attracted by jobs in Tennessee's auto plants and other growing industries. Some are drawn by Tennessee's relatively low cost of living. Some come because they like the mild climate, the beautiful scenery, and the friendly people.

Tennessee ranks seventeenth in population among the fifty states. On average, Tennessee has 116 people per square mile (45 per sq km). About 61 percent of all Tennesseans live in urban areas—towns or cities with 2,500 people or more. The remaining 39 percent live in rural areas—on farms or in small towns. The Nashville Basin area of middle Tennessee is the state's most densely populated section.

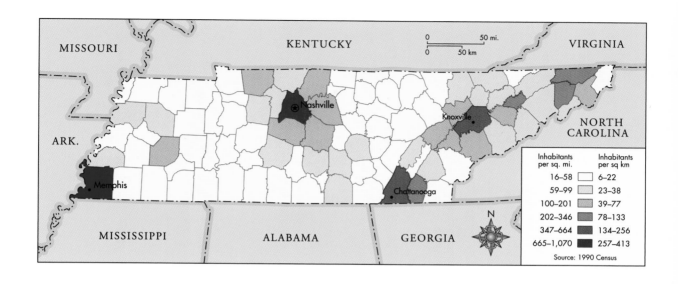

Inhabitants per sq. mi.	Inhabitants per sq km
16–58	6–22
59–99	23–38
100–201	39–77
202–346	78–133
347–664	134–256
665–1,070	257–413

Source: 1990 Census

Who Are the Tennesseans?

Approximately 83 percent of all Tennesseans are white. Many white Tennesseans are the descendants of Scotch-Irish people who crossed the mountains from Virginia and North Carolina during colonial days. Others are of English, German, French, Italian, and Eastern European ancestry.

Tennessee's population density

The Scotch-Irish

The first white settlers who made their way over the Appalachians belonged to a group called the Scotch-Irish. The Scotch-Irish had a long and complicated history. Originating in Scotland, they fled to Ireland during a series of wars. Though they lived in Ireland for nearly two centuries, they clung to their Scottish identity. Finally, they returned to Scotland, but within a few years they were driven out once more. This time they crossed the Atlantic to make a new home in North America. The Scotch-Irish settled much of the Appalachian region, from Pennsylvania to the Carolinas. ■

Hickory-Smoked Barbecue

On a clear autumn day in Memphis, smoke hangs heavy in the air. It is not the smoke of factories, but the mouth-watering fragrant smoke of Memphis's specialty—hickory-smoked barbecue. This delicacy developed during the days of slavery. As a special treat, slaves were sometimes given a freshly slaughtered pig, which they cooked slowly over a wood fire in a deep pit. When you eat pork barbecue, don't worry about getting your fingers sticky. Pick up a pork shoulder and tear the tender meat off the bone! ■

African-Americans comprise about 16 percent of Tennessee's population. Black people live in all parts of the state, but the black population is most heavily concentrated in and around Memphis. Asians make up less than 1 percent of the state's population. Hispanic people also account for less than 1 percent. Tennessee has a small Native American population. Most Indians living in Tennessee today are members of the Cherokee Nation.

If you have a good ear for accents, you will quickly learn to tell where a Tennessean comes from by the way she or he speaks. People from east Tennessee speak with a distinctive twang. West Tennesseans sound more like people from Mississippi or other parts of the Deep South.

Tennessee is sometimes said to be part of the Bible Belt. The Southern Baptist Church has a strong presence in the state, and its members believe in a literal interpretation of the Bible. Other churches in Tennessee include Methodist, Presbyterian, and Pentecostal. Roman Catholic churches stand in most cities. Jewish synagogues can be found in Nashville and Memphis.

A Tennessee fiddle maker

People of the Mountains

Tennessee's eastern mountains are part of the chain known as the Appalachians. The term *Appalachia* is sometimes used to describe mountainous parts of east Tennessee as well as portions of Kentucky, North Carolina, and West Virginia. During the 1960s, many Americans were shocked by reports of appalling poverty throughout Appalachia. Since that time, state and federal programs have improved housing, education, and health care in much of this region. Because the mountains had long isolated Appalachia from the outside world, its people play music and practice crafts that have died out in other areas. People in Tennessee's Appalachia still use some words that were common and accepted in the seventeenth century. For example, they may say "knowed" instead of "knew," "yourn" instead of "your," and "iffen" for "if." With exposure to television and radio, however, people are using these regional words less frequently. ■

The Diffusion of Knowledge

During the first decades of white settlement, Tennessee had no public schools. A few private schools sprang up to educate the children of families who could afford to pay tuition. But most Tennessee children learned to read from their parents or did not learn at all.

The constitution of 1834 declared that the state was responsible for "the diffusion of knowledge" and called for the establishment of schools for "public instruction." The first public schools served students in the elementary grades. The general assembly established public high schools in 1885. Until the 1960s, public schools in Tennessee were strictly segregated by race. The state funded two separate school systems, one for white children and one for black children.

Today, Tennessee has 651,000 elementary students and 243,000 students in secondary schools. The state spends approximately $3,800 to educate each public-school student per year.

About 37 percent of all Tennesseans have earned a college degree. Tennessee has many outstanding colleges and universities. The University of Tennessee maintains four campuses, the main one located in Knoxville. The others are in Chattanooga, Martin,

Taking notes at school

The University of Tennessee at Knoxville

and Memphis. State universities include East Tennessee State in Johnson City, Middle Tennessee State in Murfreesboro, Tennessee State University in Nashville, and Austin Peay State University in Clarksville.

In addition to its publicly funded universities, Tennessee has many private institutions of higher learning. The largest and best known of these is Vanderbilt University in Nashville, founded in 1873. Other privately run colleges include Crichton College in Memphis, University of the South in Sewanee, Tusculum University in Greeneville, and Lee University in Cleveland.

The Hunger for Learning

After the Civil War, thousands of former slaves in Tennessee were eager for education. In 1866, the Freedmen's Bureau established the Fisk Free Colored School in Nashville to teach reading, writing, and math to African-Americans of all ages. Within a year, the school had 2,000 students. The school shifted its focus in 1867 and began to train black teachers. The name was changed to Fisk University (right). Fisk is one of the oldest universities in the United States geared to the needs of black students. ■

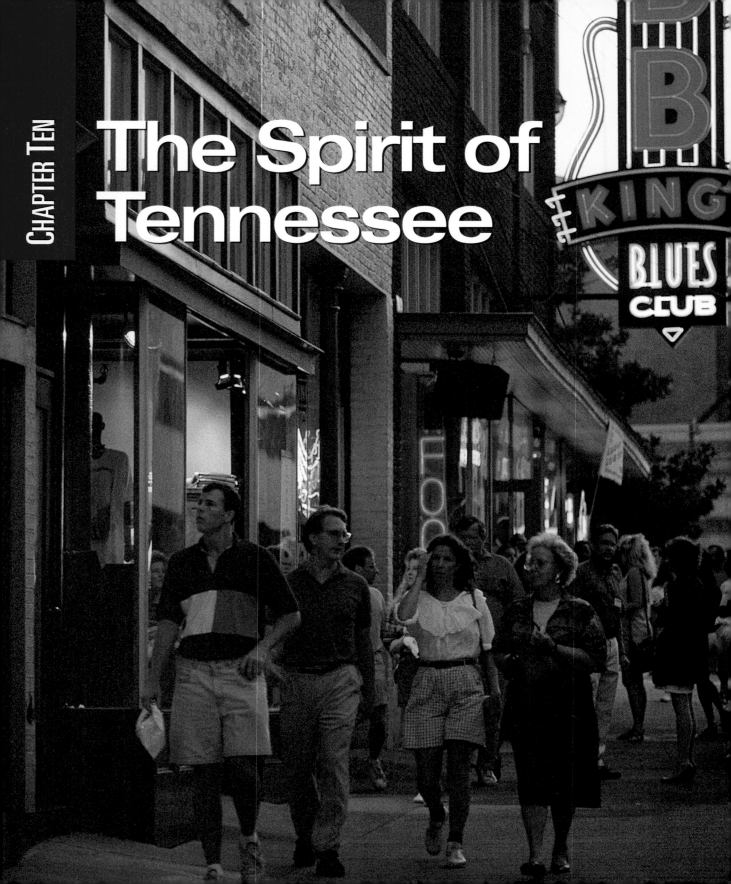

CHAPTER TEN

The Spirit of Tennessee

The highway known as I-40 stretches from Nashville to Memphis, a distance that can be covered in about three hours. Both Nashville and Memphis have made extraordinary contributions to the world of popular music. Many travelers call the road linking these unique cities "the Music Highway."

Tennessee's achievements in music go unrivaled, but music is not the state's only contribution to the arts. Tennesseans also take pride in the work of their writers, painters, and sculptors. They cheer for their athletes and participate in a variety of sports. In the realm of arts and entertainment, Tennessee is one of the stars.

Mary Noailles Murfree used the pen name Charles Egbert Craddock.

The Pen and the Paintbrush

During the frontier era, few Tennesseans had time to write novels or poetry. Writers emerged in the 1830s, when the state had become more settled. One of the first popular books to come out of Tennessee was *A Narrative of the Life of David Crockett of the State of Tennessee*, published in 1834, the frontiersman's account of his own adventures. In the 1850s, George Washington Harris (1814–1869) wrote a series of humorous sketches about Sut Lovingood, a man from the mountains of east Tennessee. Written in the dialect of the region and full of rough humor, the stories were printed in newspapers across the nation.

Opposite: Beale Street in Memphis

Two women writers depicted life in east Tennessee in the decades after the Civil War. Under the pen name Charles Egbert Craddock, Mary Noailles Murfree (1850–1922) published a collection of short stories in 1884. Murfree grew up in Murfreesboro and Nashville, in the Tennessee Mountains. She drew her settings and characters from the many summers she spent at Beersheba Springs, a resort near McMinnville. Emma Bell Miles (1879–1919), who spent much of her life in Walden's Ridge, published *The Spirit of the Mountains* in 1905. The book is a detailed description of mountain folkways, including crafts, music, food, and superstitions.

Robert Penn Warren was a professor at Vanderbilt University.

In the 1920s and 1930s, Nashville was the hub of a flourishing literary scene. Poets John Crowe Ransom (1888–1974), Allen Tate (1899–1979), and Robert Penn Warren (1905–1989) all taught at Vanderbilt University. Warren was the first writer to win the prestigious Pulitzer Prize three times. He won a Pulitzer in 1947 for his novel *All the King's Men*; in 1958, for his poetry collection *Promises*; and in 1978, for another book of poems, *Now and Then*. A number of influential African-American writers taught at Fisk University. Chief among them were James Weldon Johnson (1871–1938) and Arna Bontemps (1902–1973).

One of the most widely acclaimed Tennessee writers of the late twentieth century was Peter Taylor (1917–1994). Born in Trenton, Taylor wrote about the changes in southern life as prosperous families moved from plantations to cities. Taylor won the Pulitzer Prize in 1986 for his novel *A Summons to Memphis*. His home state is featured in his 1994 short-story collection, *In Tennessee Country*.

James Weldon Johnson taught at Fisk University.

Tennessee's first painter of note was Ralph Earl (1785?– 1838). Born in England, Earl went to Nashville to paint General Andrew Jackson in 1817. He married the niece of Jackson's wife, Rachel, and became very much part of the Jackson family. He lived at the Hermitage until Jackson was elected president and accompanied him to the White House. Earl painted dozens of portraits of Jackson, as well as pictures of his friends and relatives.

Washington Bogart Cooper (1802–1888) was the first native Tennessean to earn a reputation as a painter. Born in Jonesborough, he studied painting in Philadelphia and set up a studio in Nashville.

Roots

As he was growing up in Henning, Tennessee, Alex Haley (1921–1992) loved to listen to his grandmother and aunts tell stories of their ancestors. In 1976, Haley (left) published a book titled *Roots, the Saga of an American Family*, in which he described how he traced his family members back to Africa. He wrote of his ancestor, Kunta Kinte, who was captured by slave traders in 1767 and sold to a Virginia planter. *Roots* sold 1.5 million copies, and in 1977, it was made into an immensely popular TV miniseries. However, some scholars and critics contended that Haley had borrowed material from other writers and that his book was a hoax. Whether or not Haley's story is true, *Roots* enthralled millions of people and kindled new interest in the African-American experience. ■

He painted about thirty portraits a year over the next half-century, earning the nickname, "Man of a Thousand Portraits." James Cameron (1817–1887), a Scot by birth, came to Chattanooga in the 1830s. Cameron earned his living by painting portraits, but he is best known today for his landscapes of the Chattanooga region.

The Civil War inspired William Gilbert Gaul (1855–1919), who lived and worked in Fall Creek Falls. Gaul won awards for such action-packed paintings as *Holding the Line at All Hazard* and *Charging the Battery*. His pictures give a compassionate view of both Confederate and Union soldiers.

Another Tennessee portrait painter was Willie Betty Newman (1863–1935), who painted many of Nashville's wealthy citizens. Congress commissioned her to paint a posthumous portrait of President James K. Polk. Ella Hergesheimer (1873–1943) also had a portrait studio in Nashville. In addition to portraits, Hergesheimer painted landscapes and still lifes.

Painter Willie Betty Newman

The best-known African-American painter connected with Tennessee is Aaron Douglas (1899–1979). Born in Kansas, Douglas taught at Fisk University from the late 1930s until 1966. Many of his murals can be seen on the Fisk campus, and his works hang in museums throughout America. Douglas's work combines both European and traditional African styles, and it celebrates the role of African-Americans in the United States.

The Stingy Stonecutter

Tennessee has a long tradition of folk art, including quilting, pottery making, and basketry. One avenue for folk artists has been the carving of headstones. William Edmondson (1870–1951), an African-American from Davidson County, carved headstones with lambs, preachers, doves, and unique geometric forms. During the 1930s, the federal government strongly encouraged the work of folk artists, and Edmondson earned national recognition. In 1937, he had a one-man show at the Museum of Modern Art in New York. Edmondson described his carvings as "stingy," because he avoided any needless ornamentation. His work is simple yet powerful, using the natural contours and texture of Tennessee limestone. ■

Peyton Manning played for the Tennessee Volunteers.

Playing to Win

Pro football came to Tennessee in 1997 when the former Houston Oilers moved to Liberty Stadium in Memphis. The team soon changed its name to the Tennessee Titans. In 1999, the Titans moved to a new home stadium in Nashville.

Tennesseans are passionately loyal to the University of Tennessee football team, the Volunteers, affectionately nicknamed the Vols. In the late 1990s, the Vols achieved an incredible run of victories. Playing in the tough Southeast Conference, they had a storybook season in 1998. That year they scored thirteen straight victories and no defeats, winning the national championship. Earlier in the 1990s, the Vols were led by quarterback Peyton Manning, who was said to fire passes with the accuracy of guided missiles. After graduation, Manning starred in professional football.

The Miracle from Clarksville

Born in Clarksville, Wilma Rudolph (1940–1994) was the twentieth child in a family of twenty-two children. When she was six years old, she had a series of illnesses, including a bout with polio. She wore a metal brace on her leg until she was ten. Her mother helped her exercise every day, and slowly Wilma rebuilt her strength. By the time she was in her teens, she could not only walk again—she could run. In fact, she easily outran the fastest of her classmates. Rudolph attended Tennessee State University, where she was a member of the celebrated Tigerbelles. She went to the Olympics in 1956 and again in 1960, winning three gold medals in track and field. She was immensely popular with both U.S. and European audiences. Her accomplishments helped bring greater recognition to women's sports worldwide. ■

The most successful University of Tennessee team of all time is the Lady Volunteers Basketball Squad. Under Coach Pat Summitt, the Lady Vols won national championships in 1987, 1989, 1991, 1996, 1997, and 1998. The 1998 team was the most powerful in women's basketball history, winning all thirty-nine games it played. Coach Summitt and her Lady Vols elevated women's basketball to a major spectator sport.

One of the state's most famous college teams is the women's track team from Tennessee State University, the Tigerbelles. During the 1950s and 1960s, the Tigerbelles sent many star sprinters to the Olympic Games. Among the team's medalists were Chandra Cheeseborough, Mae Faggs, Madeline Manning, Wyomia Tyus, and Martha Watson. The brightest star of all was a charming and versatile young athlete named Wilma Rudolph.

With their long tradition of raising horses, it is not surprising that Tennesseans enjoy horse races. The Iroquois Steeplechase is a gala event in Nashville every May. Tennesseans relish all forms of outdoor activities, from swimming and boating to mountain climbing.

The Father of the Blues

W. C. Handy (1873–1958) was born in Alabama and joined a traveling minstrel band when he was only fifteen. For the next twenty years he moved from place to place—playing, composing, and listening to music across the United States and in Canada, Mexico, and Cuba. In 1908, Handy settled in Memphis to become part of the city's lively black entertainment scene. His compositions drew from many roots, including vaudeville songs, Latin rhythms, and African-American folk melodies. The campaign tune he wrote for Edward H. Crump in 1909 was later published as "Memphis Blues." Working from his home on Memphis's Beale Street, Handy published sheet music for dozens of blues songs, his own compositions and those of others. Today, the W. C. Handy House Museum is a shrine for lovers of Handy's uniquely American music. ■

A World of Music

One day in 1909, Edward H. Crump hired a musician to write a song to launch his campaign for mayor of Memphis. Crowds went wild when they heard the song at Crump's political rallies. The song, which was called "Memphis Blues," helped Crump win his election and made a name for its composer, William Christopher (W. C.) Handy. It also started a new style of music known as the blues.

The blues expressed feelings of sadness and loneliness in the eloquent dialect of African-Americans from the rural south. For decades, Memphis's Beale Street was the hub of this musical form. The street drew singers and composers from all over the South.

Musician B. B. King later described its exhilarating atmosphere: "I quickly learned that everything was happening on Beale Street. You could see people dancing in the park. You could see famous musicians just walking around, people I'd only heard of: Count Basie, Duke Ellington, Louis Jordan, people of that caliber. If you had a quarter you could get a meal that would last you all day at a place called the One-Minute Café . . . we called it 'belly-washer.' That would be your meal for a whole day."

B. B. King enjoyed the musical atmosphere of Memphis.

The Empress of the Blues

If W. C. Handy was the "Father of the Blues," Bessie Smith (1894–1937) was the Empress. Smith began her career at the age of nine, singing on the streets of Chattanooga while her brother played the guitar. Traveling to Memphis in her teens, Smith found inspiration in the work of Handy and other blues singers on Beale Street. Her best-loved songs include "Beale Street Blues," "Beale Street Mama," and "Nobody Knows You when You're Down and Out." In 1923, Smith made her first record. Its vast popularity showed recording companies that there was an eager market for music aimed at an African-American audience. Bessie Smith was a dramatic performer who swept onstage in dangling pearls and feather boas. Her booming voice carried to the streets outside the halls where she sang. ■

What Memphis is to the blues, Nashville is to country music. In 1925, a show called *Barn Dance* aired on Nashville's radio station, WSM. The first show featured an eighty-year-old fiddler named Uncle Jimmy Thompson, who promised he could "fiddle the

From Rags to Riches

Dolly Parton (1946–) was the fourth of twelve children in a sharecropping family from Sevier County. When she was only five, she began to write songs. One of her uncles helped her get an appearance on *The Grand Ole Opry* when she was thirteen. Parton moved to Nashville, where she cut numerous records, some solo and some with other performers. In the 1980s, she went to Hollywood and starred in the film *Nine to Five*. One of her most popular albums is *Here You Come Again*. In 1985, Parton opened a theme park near her Sevier County birthplace. Dollywood quickly became one of the most frequently visited theme parks in America. ■

Elvis, the King

Elvis Presley (1935–1977) did more for popular music than any other single performer. In the early 1950s, he merged the sounds of country, blues, and gospel music to help create a new form known as rock and roll. Presley was born in Tupelo, Mississippi, but moved with his family to Memphis when he was young. The Presleys were poor, but Elvis had glorious dreams of stardom. According to an often-repeated story, he walked into Sun Recording Studio in 1953 and asked to record a song as a present for his mother. Sun Studio's Sam Phillips found something special in Presley's voice and manner, and the singer's career was launched.

With his slicked-back hair and sideburns, and his swiveling motions onstage, Presley was wildly popular from 1955 through 1958. Songs such as "You Ain't Nothin' but a Hound Dog," "Love Me Tender," and "Heartbreak Hotel" are classics to this day. During the 1960s Presley starred in several Hollywood movies.

Though he made millions of dollars, his personal life was marred by tragedy. He died of complications from prescription-drug abuse at his mansion, Graceland, in 1977. Fans flock to Memphis every August to honor him during Elvis International Tribute Week. Though Elvis is gone, his legend has never died. ■

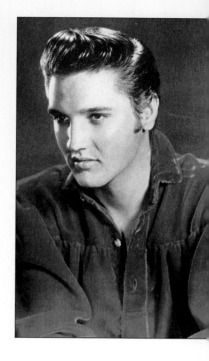

taters off the vine." Two years later, *Barn Dance* became *The Grand Ole Opry*, bringing country music into homes all across the South. *The Grand Ole Opry* was the single most powerful force in turning country music into a popular form.

Today, Nashville is known worldwide as the capital of the country- and bluegrass-music industries. Dozens of clubs in Nashville feature the top performers in the field, as well as the hopefuls who flock to the city from all over the world. Recording

A Brief Life Still Remembered

King Hiram "Hank" Williams (1923–1953) died at the age of twenty-nine, after a stunning musical career that lasted six years. Born in Alabama, he moved to Nashville to write and play country music. In 1949, he performed for the first time on *The Grand Ole Opry*, and he soon became the show's most popular entertainer. Williams wrote heartfelt songs about ordinary people leading difficult lives. His own life was troubled with chronic back pain and alcoholism. Though his performing career was short, he is still revered by country-music devotees. The Country Music Hall of Fame has a special exhibit on Williams's life and work. ■

studios offer million-dollar contracts to the most promising performers.

Country music has come a long way since Uncle Jimmy Thompson strummed his fiddle. Today's performers play amplified steel-string guitars, accompanied by bass, strings, and drums. Some still sing of the hardships and delights of life on the farm. But country songs also tell of homesickness, lonely drives on endless highways, and the joys and heartaches of love. They describe the lives of working-class Americans, but their lyrics can speak to almost anyone, anywhere.

Tennesseans also lend their strong support to classical music. Both Nashville and Memphis have acclaimed symphony orchestras. The Nashville Symphony performs in the Nashville Arts Center, which also hosts three theaters. Nashville, Memphis, and Knoxville have opera companies that play to enthusiastic audiences. Opera Memphis and the Memphis Ballet are based at the Orpheum Theater.

Whether your taste is country music or historic homes, Civil War battlefields or dazzling mountain scenery, the state of Tennessee has riches to offer. And wherever you go, the Tennesseans will make you feel welcome. No matter how much the towns and countryside may change, southern hospitality always remains the same.

Timeline

United States History

1607 The first permanent English settlement is established in North America at Jamestown.

1620 Pilgrims found Plymouth Colony, the second permanent English settlement.

1776 America declares its independence from Britain.

1783 The Treaty of Paris officially ends the Revolutionary War in America.

1787 The U.S. Constitution is written.

1803 The Louisiana Purchase almost doubles the size of the United States.

1812–15 The United States and Britain fight the War of 1812.

Tennessee State History

1540 Explorer Hernando de Soto arrives in the Cherokee town of Chiaha in present-day Tennessee.

1673 Marquette and Jolliet pass through Tennessee.

1714 Charles Charleville establishes a French trading post near present-day Nashville.

1754 The Cherokee and Chickasaw Indians finally drive the invading Shawnee out of Tennessee and across the Ohio River.

1756 British construct Fort Loudoun on the banks of the Tennessee River.

1760 Fort Loudoun surrenders to Cherokee attack.

1763 The Treaty of Paris is signed, leaving Tennessee under British control.

1775 The Treaty of Sycamore Shoals allows the Transylvania Company to purchase a large portion of Cherokee land.

1780 The Transylvania Company founds present-day Nashville; the Battle of Kings Mountain marks a turning point in the Revolutionary War.

1790 The U.S. government includes Tennessee in the Southwest Territory.

1796 Tennessee joins the Union as the sixteenth state on June 1.

1827 Tennessean Davy Crockett begins his first term as U.S. congressman.

1828 Tennessean Andrew Jackson becomes president of the United States.

United States History

The North and South fight **1861–65** each other in the American Civil War.

The United States is **1917–18** involved in World War I.

The stock market crashes, **1929** plunging the United States into the Great Depression.

The United States **1941–45** fights in World War II.
The United States becomes a **1945** charter member of the U.N.

The United States **1951–53** fights in the Korean War.

The U.S. Congress enacts a series of **1964** groundbreaking civil rights laws.

The United States **1964–73** engages in the Vietnam War.

The United States and other **1991** nations fight the brief Persian Gulf War against Iraq.

Tennessee State History

1830 Sequoyah begins developing the Cherokee language's written form. Andrew Jackson signs the Indian Removal Act, forcing the Cherokee to give up their land in Tennessee.

1838 U.S. troops force the Cherokee to march from Tennessee to Oklahoma in the Trail of Tears.

1839 James K. Polk becomes governor of Tennessee.

1861 Tennessee joins the Confederate States of America on June 8.

1866 Tennessee becomes the first Confederate state to be readmitted to the Union on July 24.

1933 Franklin D. Roosevelt creates the Tennessee Valley Authority.

1945 Tennessean Cordell Hull wins the Nobel Peace Prize.

1968 James Earl Ray assassinates Martin Luther King Jr. in Memphis on April 4.

1976 Al Gore is elected to the U.S. Congress.

2000 Al Gore is nominated to be the Democratic candidate for president.

Fast Facts

Statehood date	June 1, 1796, the 16th state
Origin of state name	*Tenasie* was the name of a Cherokee village on the Tennessee River. From 1784 to 1788, the area was called Franklin or Frankland
State capital	Nashville
State nicknames	Volunteer State; Big Bend State
State motto	*Agriculture and commerce*
State bird	Mockingbird
State flower	Iris
State wildflower	Passionflower
State fish	Large mouth bass
State animal	Raccoon
State songs	"My Homeland, Tennessee," "When It's Iris Time in Tennessee," "Tennessee Waltz," "My Tennessee," and "Rocky Top"
State tree	Tulip poplar
State fair	September at Nashville
Total area; rank	42,146 sq. mi. (109,158 sq km); 36th
Land; rank	41,220 sq. mi. (106,760 sq km); 34th
Water; rank	926 sq. mi. (2,398 sq km); 30th
***Inland water;* rank**	926 sq. mi. (2,398 sq km); 24th

State capitol

Pyramid Arena in Memphis

Geographic center	Rutherford County, 5 miles (8 km) northeast of Murfreesboro
Latitude and longitude	Tennessee is located approximately between 35° and 36° 41' N and 81° 0' and 90° 18' W
Highest point	Clingmans Dome, 6,643 feet (2,026 m)
Lowest point	In Shelby County, 182 feet (56 m)
Largest city	Memphis
Number of towns	95
Population; rank	4,896,641 (1990 census); 17th
Density	116 persons per sq. mi. (45 per sq km)
Population distribution	61% urban, 39% rural

Ethnic distribution (does not equal 100%)

White	83.0%
African-American	15.95%
Hispanic	0.67%
Asian and Pacific Islanders	0.65%
Native American	0.21%
Other	0.19%

Record high temperature	113°F (45°C) at Perryville on July 29 and August 9, 1930
Record low temperature	–32°F (–36°C) at Mountain View on December 30, 1917
Average July temperature	78°F (26°C)
Average January temperature	38°F (3°C)
Average annual precipitation	52 inches (132 cm)

Smoky Mountains

Natural Areas and Historic Sites

National Park

Great Smoky Mountains National Park is on the North Carolina–Tennessee border covering more than 521,000 acres (211,005 ha).

National Scenic Trail

Appalachian National Scenic Trail is a 2,158-mile (3,473-km) trail extending the length of the Appalachians from Maine to Georgia.

Natchez Trace Parkway National Scenic Trail is a 694-mile (1,117-km)-long trail that follows the Natchez Trace Parkway.

National Recreation Area

Big South Fork National River and National Recreation Area preserves a free-flowing fork of the Cumberland River and provides fine recreational facilities with natural and historical features.

National Military Park

Chickamauga and Chattanooga National Military Park preserves Civil War battle sites. Parts of the park are located in Georgia.

Shiloh National Military Park is the site of a major Civil War battle in 1862. The park also contains the Shiloh Indian Mounds National Historical Landmark.

National Historic Site

Andrew Johnson National Historic Site preserves two homes and the tailor shop of the seventeenth president of the United States. The site also encompasses the Andrew Johnson National Cemetery.

National Historical Park

Cumberland Gap National Historical Park commemorates the mountain pass in the Appalachian Mountains that was an important route for westward settlers. Parts of the park lie in Virginia and Kentucky.

National Wild and Scenic River

Obed National Wild and Scenic River preserves deep gorges and rugged scenery that provide exciting recreational possibilities.

Cumberland Gap

National Battlefield

Fort Donelson National Battlefield commemorates the site of the first major Union army victory in the Civil War in 1862.

Stones River National Battlefield was the site of a fierce midwinter battle during the Civil War.

Sports Teams

NCAA Teams (Division 1)

Austin Peay State University Governors

East Tennessee State University Buccaneers

Middle Tennessee State University Blue Raiders

Tennessee State University Tigers

Tennessee Tech University Golden Eagles

University of Memphis Tigers

University of Tennessee–Chattanooga Moccasins

University of Tennessee–Knoxville Volunteers

University of Tennessee–Martin Skyhawks

Vanderbilt University Commodores

National Football League

Tennessee Titans

Peyton Manning

Cultural Institutions

Libraries

The State Library and Archives (Nashville) holds important collections on Tennessee history, literature, biography, as well as state and federal documents.

The Vanderbilt University Library (Nashville) and the *University of Tennessee Library* (Knoxville) both have important academic and scholarly collections.

University of
Tennessee

Museums

The Tennessee State Museum (Nashville) features exhibits on the state's history.

The Cumberland Science Museum (Nashville) has a planetarium, as well as exhibits on science, natural history, and culture.

The National Civil Rights Museum (Memphis) is housed in the former motel where Martin Luther King Jr. was assassinated.

The Country Music Hall of Fame and Museum (Nashville) commemorates the rich musical traditions of Nashville.

The Carl Van Vechten Museum of Art at Knoxville University houses important collections of art by African-Americans.

Performing Arts

Tennessee has three major opera companies, four major symphony orchestras, and one major dance company.

Universities and Colleges

In the late 1990s, Tennessee had twenty-four public and fifty-two private institutions of higher learning.

Annual Events

January–March

Eagle-watch tours at Reelfoot Lake near Tiptonville (January–March)

National Field Trial Championships for bird dogs in Grand Junction (February)

April–June

Dogwood Arts Festival in Knoxville (April)

Spring Wildflower Pilgrimage in Gatlinburg (April)

East Tennessee Strawberry Festival in Dayton (May)

Iroquois Steeplechase in Nashville (May)

Festival of British and Appalachian Culture in Rugby (May)

Memphis in May International Festival (May)

Tennessee coneflower

International Country Music Fan Fair in Nashville (June)

Riverbend Festival in Chattanooga (June)

Rhododendron Festival in Roan Mountain (June)

July–September
Frontier Days in Lynchburg (July)

Old Time Fiddlers' Jamboree and Crafts Festival in Smithville (July)

International Grand Championship Walking Horse Show in Murfreesboro (August)

Agriculture and Industrial Fair in Knoxville (September)

The Mid-South Fair in Memphis (September)

October–December
National Storytelling Festival in Jonesborough (October)

Autumn Gold Festival in Coker Creek (October)

Oktoberfest in Memphis (October)

Fall Color Cruise and Folk Festival in Chattanooga (October)

Fall Craftsman's Fair in Gatlinburg (October)

Davy Crockett

Famous People

David (Davy) Crockett (1786–1836)	Frontiersman and public official
David Glasgow Farragut (1801–1870)	Naval officer
Albert Gore Jr. (1948–)	Politician
Alex Haley (1921–1992)	Writer
Cordell Hull (1871–1955)	Public official
Andrew Jackson (1767–1845)	U.S. president
Andrew Johnson (1808–1875)	U.S. president
Dolly Parton (1946–)	Singer and actor
Elvis Presley (1935–1977)	Singer and actor
Wilma Rudolph (1940–1994)	Olympic athlete
Alvin Cullum York (1887–1964)	Soldier

To Find Out More

History

- Chambers, Catherine E. *Tennessee*. New York: Benchmarks Books, 1997.

- Fradin, Dennis Brindell. *Tennessee*. Chicago: Childrens Press, 1992.

- Sirvaitis, Karen. *Tennessee*. Minneapolis: Lerner, 1991.

- Thompson, Kathleen. *Tennessee*. Austin, Tex.: Raintree/Steck-Vaughn, 1996.

Biography

- Crockett, David. *Davy Crockett: His Own Story: A Narrative of the Life of David Crockett of the State of Tennessee*. New York: Applewood, 1993.

- Moseley, Elizabeth R. *Davy Crockett: Hero of the Wild Frontier*. New York: Chelsea, 1991.

Fiction

- Allen, Thomas B. *On Granddaddy's Farm*. New York: Knopf, 1989.

- Crist-Evans, Craig. *Moon over Tennessee: A Boy's Civil War Journal*. Boston: Houghton Mifflin, 1999.

- Giovanni, Nikki T. *Knoxville, Tennessee*. New York: Scholastic, 1994.

- Rabinowitz, Sandy. *Changing Times: The Story of a Tennessee Walking Horse and the Girl Who Proves That Grown-Ups Don't Always Know Best*. New York: Scholastic, 1998.

Website

- **State of Tennessee**
  http://www.state.tn.us/
  The official website for the
  state of Tennessee

Addresses

- **Information Center**
  Tennessee State Capitol
  Nashville, TN 37219
  For information on
  Tennessee's government

- **Department of Tourist
  Development**
  P.O. Box 23170
  Nashville, TN 37202
  For information on
  Tennessee's tourism and
  history

- **Department of Economic
  and Community
  Development**
  Industrial Research Division
  320 Sixth Avenue N.
  Nashville, TN 37219
  For information on
  Tennessee's economy

Index

Page numbers in *italics* indicate illustrations.

Meet the Author

Deborah Kent grew up in Little Falls, New Jersey, where she was the first totally blind student to attend the local public school. She received a B.A. in English from Oberlin College and earned a master's degree from Smith College School for Social Work. For four years, she worked in community mental health at the University Settlement House on New York City's Lower East Side.

In 1975, Ms. Kent left social work to pursue her dream of becoming a writer. She moved to San Miguel de Allende, Mexico, a town with a thriving colony of foreign writers and artists. In San Miguel, she wrote her first book, *Belonging*, a novel for young adults. She also helped to establish the Centro de Crecimiento, a school for children with disabilities.

Ms. Kent is the author of fifteen young-adult novels and many nonfiction books for children. She lives in Chicago with her husband, children's author R. Conrad Stein, and their daughter, Janna.

As she worked on this book, Deborah Kent enjoyed talking to Tennesseeans about their state's history and lore. She would love to explore further Tennessee's mountains, forests, and historic sites.

Photo Credits

Photographs ©:

AP/Wide World Photos: 91 top (Chris O'Meara), 48, 49, 86, 91 bottom, 116, 121, 125
Buddy Mays/Travel Stock: back cover
Byron Jorjorian: 66 top, 134 bottom
Corbis-Bettmann: 120, 133 (AFP), 35 (The Corcoran Gallery of Art), 22 (Raymond Gehman), 17 (Hulton-Deutsch Collection), 123 (Peter Josek/Reuters), 41 (Minnesota Historical Society), 126 (Penguin), 40, 51, 101 (UPI), 18, 24, 31, 34, 38, 117, 124 top, 135
Delimont, Herbig & Associates: 58, 132 bottom (Adam Jones), 132 bottom, 6 top right, 54, 93 (Scott T. Smith)
Envision/Steven Needham: 97
Liaison Agency, Inc.: 33 top, 118, 124 bottom (Hulton Getty), 86 top (Bob Schatz)
Mary Liz Austin: 2
New England Stock Photo: 7 top right, 111 (Robert Boyer), 71 (Andre Jenny), 7 bottom, 109 (Frank Siteman)
North Wind Picture Archives: 14, 16, 75 (N. Carter), 25, 28, 29, 30, 43, 44, 45

Paul Edelstein Gallery, Memphis, TN: 119 bottom
Photri/Leonard Lee Rue III: 67
Richard W. Clark: 6 top center, 12, 55, 65
State of Tennessee Photographic Services: 6 bottom, 9, 13, 39, 53, 60, 64, 68, 70, 73, 79, 80, 82, 83, 88 top, 88 bottom left, 88 bottom right, 90 right, 94, 95, 96, 104, 105, 106, 130, 131
Stock Montage, Inc.: 20, 21, 36, 37, 46, 122
Stone/Chad Ehlers: 7 top left, 76
Tennessee State Library and Archive: 50, 115, 119 top
Terry Livingstone: 63, 74 top, 102
Tom Till: cover, 8, 57, 132 top
Unicorn Stock Photos: 114 (Florent Flipper), 112, 134 top (Joseph L. Fontenot), 69, 78, 100 (Jeff Greenberg), 113 (Jean Higgins), 81, 99 (Scott Liles), 6 top left, 92 (Robin Rudd)
Visuals Unlimited/Jeff Greenberg: 7 top center, 72
Woolaroc Museum, Bartlesville, OK: 33 bottom ("Trail of Tears", by Robert Lindneux)
Maps by: XNR Productions, Inc.